Tadaima! I Am Home

FVB
362 1/13/24 Seat 10A

Cindy
Visit to Honolulu
Jan 2024
Sylvia

INTERSECTIONS

Asian and Pacific American Transcultural Studies

RUSSELL C. LEONG
DAVID K. YOO
Series Editors

Tadaima! I Am Home
A Transnational Family History

Tom Coffman

University *of* Hawai'i Press

HONOLULU

In association with
UCLA Asian American Studies Center, Los Angeles

23 22 21 20 19 18   6 5 4 3 2 1

Library of Congress Cataloging-in-Publication Data

Coffman, Tom.
Names: Coffman, Tom, author.
Title: Tadaima! I am home : a transnational family history / Tom Coffman.
Other titles: Intersections (Honolulu, Hawaii)
Description: Honolulu : University of Hawai'i Press ; Los Angeles : in
    association with UCLA Asian American Studies Center, [2018] | Series:
    Intersections : Asian and Pacific American transcultural studies |
    Includes bibliographical references and index.
Identifiers: LCCN 2018008662| ISBN 9780824876647 (cloth ; alk. paper) | ISBN
    9780824877279 (pbk. ; alk. paper)
Subjects: LCSH: Miwa family. | Japanese
    Americans—Hawaii—Honolulu—Biography. | Transnationalism—Case studies.
    | Hiroshima-shi (Japan)—Emigration and immigration—Case studies. |
    Honolulu (Hawaii)—Emigration and immigration—Case studies.
Classification: LCC E184.J3 C63 2019 | DDC 973/.04956—dc23
LC record available at https://lccn.loc.gov/2018008662

Cover art: Fumio Lawrence Miwa's middle school class photo, Kure, Hiroshima,
1946; James Seigo Miwa and family in front of the main J. S. Miwa Building,
Honolulu, Hawai'i, 1932; Fumio Lawrence's August 6, 1945, diary entry. Miwa
Family Collection.

CONTENTS

List of Names · **vii**

Preface · **ix**

I THE ANCESTORS

1 A Samurai's Journey to Hawai'i · **3**

2 The Merchant's Story · **12**

II BETWEEN

3 Turning a Profit · **23**

4 Interned by the USA · **45**

5 Traded to Japan · **61**

III IN JAPAN

6 Coming of Age in Hiroshima · **83**

7 A Schoolboy's Diary · **96**

8 The Explosion of Home · **110**

IV HOME

9 *Tadaima* in America · **127**

Epilogue · **147**

Notes · **149**

Sources · **153**

Index · **157**

LIST OF NAMES

Marujiro Miwa (1850–1919), born a samurai, eventually a sojourner to plantation Hawai'i. Father of Senkichi Miwa.

Senkichi Miwa (1871–1937), briefly a Hawai'i plantation laborer, then a storekeeper and inventive entrepreneur. Father of James Seigo Miwa.

James Seigo Miwa (1897–1954), also widely known as J. S. Miwa, and as Seigo or Shogo Miwa. Transnational entrepreneur. Father of Lawrence Fumio Miwa.

Lawrence Fumio Miwa, b. 1931, known in Hawai'i as Larry Miwa and in Japan as Fumio Miwa. Securities and bank executive. Father of Stephen H. Miwa.

Stephen H. Miwa, b. 1963, family historian.

Katherine Kiyoko Miwa, (1923–2018), and Shozo Miwa, b. 1926, siblings of Lawrence Miwa.

Binjiro Kudo, (1897–1976), onetime acting consul general of Japan in Honolulu, golfing partner of James Seigo Miwa and eventual father-in-law of Lawrence F. Miwa.

Much of Stephen Miwa's life was not unlike many other people's. He had grown up in material comfort in the suburbs of Honolulu, attended public school, and engaged in such conventions as playing baseball. He moved on to the University of Hawai'i, from which he graduated with a degree in liberal arts. He thought of becoming a counselor but instead fell into marketing office systems. He did well, thanks—I imagine—to his good character and genuine capacity for friendship. He married his high school sweetheart, and together they lived in the suburbs. Stephen and Carrie had one child, a daughter named Chloe. None of which explained his extraordinary quest to retrieve the Miwa family's past.

The seed of his quest dated to a remark of his mother, who had said, mysteriously, that the Miwa family was unlucky. Just why, she was reluctant to say. At the time, Stephen was a teenager. He had turned to an aunt. "What does that mean?" he asked, " 'The Miwas are unlucky'?" The aunt had replied by asking, "Are you sure you want to know?"

These few words germinated over decades. When his mother died, Stephen was thirty-six years old. He set aside a little money, with which he took time out to explore the meaning of his mother's line, "The Miwas are unlucky." He stayed up late, combed the internet, and bought a shelf full of books.

Previously his father, Lawrence F. Miwa, had brushed aside Stephen's inquiries. Now Lawrence was in his late seventies. By asking him more informed questions, Stephen began to get answers. Lawrence told him stories and also shared dense files that he had not otherwise revisited in an adult life of forging ahead.

Key documents were in Japanese, so Stephen recruited a translator at the Japanese Cultural Center of Hawai'i, who adapted selected pieces into English. Two stood out. One was a family genealogy that went back to the 1850s. The second was a diary that Lawrence had kept as a teenager in Hiroshima, Japan, in the late summer and early autumn of 1945.

Part way through this exploration, brimming with ideas, Stephen telephoned me for a get-acquainted meeting. He appeared at my door wearing a large smile and aviator-style eyeglasses, and bearing a box of treats and a bag filled with research materials of varying pertinence. As a result of my writing life in Hawai'i, I had researched Japanese immigrants who had settled and given birth to the storied *Nisei* generation of Japanese Americans. I was aware of a lesser number who had moved on to the United States continent, and of fewer still who had returned to the folds of Japan, not to be heard from again.

Now the multiple generations of the Miwa genealogy presented a fourth category of migration. They were a transnational family who had tried, through thick and thin, to make a life in both Japan and the United States, more or less simultaneously. They had traveled often between Hiroshima and Honolulu, and occasionally on to San Francisco, developing businesses as they went.

I was excited by the story's possibilities, which in the abstract I saw as multigenerational and transnational, and which in closer view was agonizingly human. I nonetheless was apprehensive that the narrative would be impossibly difficult to locate, particularly the research that would be required in Japan.

As I thought about what I might be capable (or incapable) of writing, I began to randomly sketch the Miwa history in conversation. In the throes of such nattering, I encountered two researchers from Japan in the Hawai'i State Archives. Dr. Kosuke Harayama was curator of the interwar exhibit of the Japan National History Museum; his associate Kaori Akiyama was working on a doctorate in and out of Honolulu in Japanese American Studies. I asked if we might talk, and they said yes, definitely, and that by chance I was on their list of people to contact that week. Serendipity was at work. At closing time, we walked to a nearby bar. They turned out to be especially interested in transnational migration, and they volunteered to instruct me in how to access archives in Japan, as well as to tutor me on other resources.

I decided to quickly act on their generous offer while it was fresh in their minds. Stephen was unavailable to travel, but I nonetheless booked a flight.

PER INSTRUCTION, I LANDED AT NARITA Airport and took the train to a semi-rural area called Chiba. From Narita, it is situated in the opposite direction from Tokyo and, somewhat strangely, is the location of Japan's only national history museum. After several days of orientation in its excellent galleries under the guidance of Dr. Harayama, he and I and Kaori boarded the *Shinkansen* south. On previous trips, I had bypassed

Hiroshima, but now the reflexes of work provided me with a kind of protective shield.

Most superficially, Hiroshima emerged as a city of uniformly new buildings and numerous monuments. First, we went to the Hiroshima City archives. In an open-and-shut manner, the archivists pulled up various materials that bore directly or indirectly on the Miwas' old neighborhood, which was the Yokogawa District of the city. The material was remarkable, but the meeting itself was brief and perfunctory. We took a photograph with the staff to mark the moment and went on about our business.

From the archives, we caught a city trolley that reaches a dead end in the pedestrian plaza of Yokogawa. We wandered the streets, looking for where the Miwas had lived during their most prosperous period. Dr. Harayama, equipped with an iPad, walked about consulting his global positioning software. Clearly, the onetime Miwa Street was one block over from the *old* Yokogawa bridge and two blocks from the *new* Yokogawa bridge that runs into the plaza.

Kaori proposed that we look in the shops for people who might have known the Miwas, or at least known of them. She engaged various elderly people in conversation, and Dr. Harayama tapped away on his iPad. I stood around smiling faintly. *Sumimasen*. Excuse me.

We found a man in a shop so piled with goods that locating a specific piece of anything must have been a great chore. He was a handsome old man with wavy iron-gray hair. He nodded and said he would make a telephone call—I was not clear to whom. It turned out to be his sister, who had heard of Stephen's great grandfather, Senkichi Miwa. Senkichi, she affirmed, was an important man. I was reminded of Stephen's vignette, that when Senkichi died, his son—Stephen's grandfather—organized an old-style funeral parade of wailing mourners and snorting horses.

We found a second scrap of memory via a charming woman in her sixties who owned a small produce store near the rail line that runs through Yokogawa. Her storefront was situated on a side street that was quiet enough to jaywalk safely. She had heard of Senkichi Miwa from older family members. As if to validate the accuracy of her memory, she brought out a photograph of a prewar Japanese wooden building that had served the neighborhood as a credit union. With a fine smile, she held the picture while I photographed it. I then photographed it with her, then her and the picture with Kaori and Kosuke—a happy moment.

Yokogawa swelters in midday in July, but the heat abates in late afternoon, and the air is filled with a feeling of renewal. With the sun setting, we wandered into the world of red lanterns, grilled seafood, and *biiru*, and there we attempted to collect our thoughts. I was reassured. What might be learned about the multiple generations of a particular transnational family? What might be learned *from* them?

Tadaima! I Am Home

PART I

The Ancestors

CHAPTER ONE
A Samurai's Journey to Hawai'i

Stephen Miwa gracefully separated himself from the millions who claim samurai ancestors by saying that his great-great-grandfather Marujiro was a samurai of low rank. By accident of unfortunate timing, Marujiro was born a samurai in the age of impending modernization. According to the village register, Marujiro was born in 1850 in the mountains above the coastal town of Hiroshima. Presumably his loyalties at birth were to the lord of Hiroshima Castle, which in 1850 had stood for about two hundred and fifty years.

Marujiro was three years old when Commodore Matthew Perry navigated his Black Ships into the harbor at Yokohama, demonstrating the power of the steam engine, cannon, and, more generally, the power of America. He was eighteen at the start of the Meiji Era, arriving at manhood only to find that the way of the sword had been displaced by the way of the gun.

Estimates of the number of samurai set adrift in Hiroshima by the Meiji regime range from several thousand to as high as twenty thousand. This was not all that unusual: in the Satsuma region of the southern island, Kyushu, with an extraordinary warrior tradition, as much as one fifth of the population was samurai. Scholars are almost uniformly agreed that in the upheaval of modernization, no class was more adversely affected than the samurai, pushed out as they were into the cold world of industrialization.

Marujiro was not only without traditional status but was also a second-born son. At age twenty he married a woman named Kayo Miwa, who was eighteen. Marujiro's name was originally Omura Marujiro. He became Miwa Marujiro, taking his wife's name as a means of perpetuating the Miwa family line. This was a common practice, which in his instance was tied to a durable family house in his and Kayo's mountain village, Furuichi.

Furuichi was about ten kilometers north of Hiroshima town, lying along the road that connected the prefectures of Hiroshima and Shimane, on the opposite side of Honshu Island. Furuichi sat on the forested mountainside that was part of a large half-circle surrounding and protecting Hiroshima Castle. This natural amphitheater was strategically located, in that it was at a point where the east–west line of Honshu Island bent to the south. Stream waters cascaded from the surrounding bowl, creating the Ota River, which is an unusually large river, even for water-rich Japan. Over vast time, the Ota River had deposited topsoil from the mountains, building a broad delta that was favorable for human habitation. The accreted soil formed islands that, on the flat, split the river into branches, each with its own name. One branch split into two, and one branch split several times. The result was seven fingers of gorgeous wide rivers, all of them running through Hiroshima into the sea.

Nature was kind. The offshore waters were dotted by a diversity of small islands, forming a channel. On the far side of the channel was Shikoku Island, the shield of the Inland Sea. From this, Hiroshima enjoyed a protected waterway and productive fisheries, as well as abundant fresh water and fertile farmlands. Its inhabitants could readily feed themselves on the crucial combination of protein and carbohydrates, and they participated in coastal and interisland trade.

Taken together, the mountains, the multiple rivers, and the offshore islands made Hiroshima not only particularly livable but defensible. The successive lords of Hiroshima Castle must have been tempted to remain a world unto themselves, but the modernization movement required that parochial interests be subordinated to a new national interest. In the storied evolution of Japan to nationhood, Hiroshima became a stronghold of southern Honshu, the main island of Japan's four core islands. Like a sentinel, it guarded the western end of the Inland Sea, which led to Osaka and beyond to Yokohama and Edo, where Perry had anchored.

The sovereignty of Hiroshima Castle and the special status of the samurai fell in tandem. As suddenly as Marujiro had lost status, Japan became a more cohesive nation. To soften the fall, the national government initially gave pensions to the samurai, but soon the lower-ranking ones were categorized as commoners. The pensions of those such as Marujiro were effectively cut off altogether by a forced austerity policy in the mid-1880s. To be a low-ranking samurai was to be out of luck and out of money.

The countryside, of which the village of Furuichi was a part, disproportionately financed the universities, factories, trains, and ships of the new order. Four-fifths of the government's revenue was derived from land taxes. The government dedicated one-eighth of these taxes to capital formation while saving another eighth—an exercise of frugality unimaginable in later times.[1] Where the closed Japan had a stable population, the population of modernizing Japan began to grow rapidly. With this came a deeply held fear that the country's resources would be overrun. This was more than an imaginary problem in Hiroshima, where the pressure of numbers caused family farm plots to shrink to less than two acres.

While such trends were occurring on a grand scale, Marujiro fathered eight children. The evidence of his financial struggle is ironclad: he left Japan to work as a laborer.

As Japan began to look outward, the King of Hawai'i, His Majesty David Kalākaua, unexpectedly arrived in Japan. The year was 1881. Kalākaua was on the first reach of his famous journey around the Earth, landing in Yokohama Harbor. He initially thought of himself as traveling incognito, but word of his presence spread. The cannons of the many ships in port roared a great welcome, and a band played *Hawai'i Pono'ī*, the anthem that he himself had written for his mid-Pacific nation.

The King broke out his royal uniform and ran up his royal colors. Four princes of Japan greeted him, then hurried him off to meet the Meiji emperor. Kalākaua was the embodiment of the spirit of *aloha*, by which all people were connected to one another. In this capacity, Kalākaua did the unthinkable: he shook the Meiji's hand. The next day he was escorted by a train of twenty-eight carriages to the Imperial Theater. A thousand lanterns burned, each exhibiting the flag of Japan and the royal imprint of Hawai'i. "On the stage our travelers saw fairies floating through the air like butterflies," Kalākaua's companion wrote, "and a terrific giant fighting with about fifty warriors; and his Majesty was delighted with the oddity and marvelous variety of the performance."

The women made a strong impression, "having very fair, pearly and transparent complexions, with high arched eyebrows, a great sweetness and beauty of expression, and dressed very tastefully in soft, yet brilliant silks; and with a dazzling sparkle of brilliants around their beautiful necks, and in the lobes of their shell tinted ears."

On the surface all was well with Kalākaua, but his appearance of great confidence was somewhat of a front. He knew, as his hosts likely did not, that the future of his nation was threatened by the growing influence of Americans. From within his country there was the incessant pressure of the American missionary descendants, who were now in the sugar business, and from without was the pressure of American expansionists, who were attracted to the deep-water harbor on Oʻahu formed by the Puʻuloa River—to become known to the world as Pearl Harbor. The missionary descendants of Hawaiʻi wanted free access to the American sugar market, and the Americans wanted Puʻuloa.

With the most powerful figures of Japan in his reach, Kalākaua improvised. He proposed that Japan allow its citizens to emigrate to Hawaiʻi. Further, he proposed that a prince of Japan marry a particularly desirable princess of the Hawaiian Kingdom, the goddess-like Kaʻiulani. Finally, he suggested that the emperor create an alliance of Asian nations as a counterweight to America's domineering behavior.

The emperor poured choice champagne, a gift of the emperor of Russia. He awarded Kalākaua a prestigious medal. Kalākaua in turn presented the emperor with the Grand Cross of Kamehameha, the founding father of the Hawaiian nation.

The emperor said that if he were to presume to lead a Pacific alliance, the Chinese dynasty would balk. He likewise tactfully declined the idea of a royal marriage.

The emigration of Japanese workers to Hawaiʻi was a different matter. In the account of these pleasant exchanges, the writer who accompanied Kalākaua inserted an awkward but striking non sequitur: "Hawaii is placed under deep obligation to Japan," the word obligation apparently being code for the sense of mutuality that might unlock the door of the cloistered Japanese nation. Emigration was a live subject.

Previously, in the first year of Emperor Meiji's reign, a single ship of adventurous Japanese had sailed to Hawaiʻi without government approval. Thereafter, the crude conditions of the Hawaiʻi plantations and the shabby treatment of Japanese labor had inhibited further emigration, but now it had become more attractive. Emigrants could send money home, which would shore up the rural economy. Emigration might not only help finance the modernization movement but also help Japan get a better understanding of the outside world, from which it had been isolated for so long.

After Kalākaua departed, the courtship continued. The Hawaiian consul presented a velvet curtain for the Imperial Theater that celebrated the second month of the year 2541 (Japanese era), thereby paying respect to the mythological idea that Japan was born of the Sun Goddess Amaterasu in ancient times. For the Kingdom of Hawai'i, the story of Amaterasu posed no metaphysical problem. Hawai'i itself, according to its creation chant, had been born in the time when steam poured forth from the Earth like sweat, when Sky Father had coupled with Earth Mother, after which one hundred generations of Hawaiian people had followed.

Meiji Japan and the Kingdom of Hawai'i concluded a labor pact defining the conditions of work. This pact was the first of repeated indications that Japan intended to keep a hand on the emigrants—*Japan's* emigrants—and to measure Japan's national prestige by how well its overseas workers were treated.

By 1885, four years after Kalākaua's royal visit, the stage was set for recruiting workers from rural Japan for their great adventure. At the time, the newly industrialized textile mills of Tokyo were trolling for workers in the central part of the island of Honshu. The Hawaiian consul was a labor recruiter, Robert Irwin. Irwin swung to the south, recruiting people from southern Honshu and across the Inland Sea in Kyushu. In the process, Irwin set off what would be remembered in Japan as *Hawai'i netsu,* a fever for Hawai'i. Twenty-eight thousand

King David Kalākaua, 1881.
(Hawai'i State Archives)

people competed for just over six hundred places in the first major shipment of workers. Most of them hoped to make money and send part of it home to their struggling families, but not to settle.

By this time, the medieval fiefdoms of Japan had been reorganized into units of a national government. The city of Hiroshima and its surrounding areas—the town of Furuichi, the delta, the rivers, the islands, and the adjacent lands in all directions—were now Hiroshima Prefecture. Irwin personally recruited plantation workers in Hiroshima, on the recommendation of a Japanese associate who had served as a marriage go-between to the parents of Irwin's Japanese wife.

The abundance of nature had created an abundance of workers. As the migrants departed into the unknown, the governor of Hiroshima told them, "Save money and return home in glory." The wages sent back to Japan built irrigation systems, schools, and family homes that were, in the words of Hiroshima's governor, "grand houses surrounded by walls of white mortar."[2] The total amount of money sent home by workers in a year was equal to more than half of the Hiroshima prefectural budget.

As more and more land in Hawai'i was consumed by plantations, the demand for low-cost foreign labor increased. Thanks substantially to the large number of workers from Hiroshima Prefecture, the Japanese component of Hawai'i's multiracial workforce went from virtually nothing to nearly two-thirds of all overseas workers within a few years. In the single year 1894, the output of Hawai'i's sugar industry grew from 150,000 tons to 220,000 tons, and it was in this context that Miwa Marujiro of Furuichi was swept into the Pacific current.

By this time, the government-to-government system had become a sort of Wild West operation. On the Japanese end, the supplying of labor was dominated by private Japanese emigration companies. On the Hawai'i end it was dominated by the erratic performance of the American-supported coup d'état government. As this occurred, the narrative of the workers' adventure began to give way to a narrative of hardship and suffering.

The planters specified, "The laborers shall be young, able bodied, healthy, agricultural laborers...." Further, lest there be doubt on this point, "(workers) shall under no circumstances be taken from the inhabitants of towns or cities, or be from among persons engaged or trained in pursuits other than agricultural." They were to be strong farm boys.

By these measures, Marujiro was recruited from the bottom of the heap. Where most of the recruits were in their late teens or their twenties, Marujiro was forty-four years old, which then was past the average life expectancy of a male in Japan. Further, Marujiro was not a peasant farmer, which the planters wanted, but a displaced warrior. He nursed a memory of better times. He also aspired to a better future than plantation labor—he was, by virtue of marriage, in line to be the headman of the Miwa family. For all these reasons, his journey to Hawai'i suggested a moment of desperation.

MARUJIRO SAILED FROM KOBE, JAPAN, IN late 1894 on the S.S. *Beutala*, a British cargo ship that was powered by a combination of steam engines and a two-masted sailing rig. At the time, Japan had no such ships of its own. It was trying to buy ships from Britain. The *Beutala* arrived in Honolulu on January 3, 1895, dropping anchor along the reef that protected Honolulu Harbor from incoming storms, connecting to a catwalk that led to the Customs House.

Labor recruiters said Hawai'i was *tengoku,* a paradise on Earth, but the Hawai'i of Marujiro's encounter was in turmoil. Kalākaua had died three years previously. He was succeeded by his sister, Lili'uokalani, who then was dethroned by American-descended white planters who had conspired with the United States Navy. The American missionary descendant Sanford Dole and his cohorts claimed legitimacy by virtue of their occupation of key public buildings, such as 'Iolani Palace, the Royal Barracks, the legislative building, the Opera House, and the Customs House.

By coincidence, Marujiro arrived the day that Native Hawaiian rebels landed a shipment of guns near Diamond Head. In their hope of mounting a counterrevolution, they were soon to be confronted by missionary militia, who were heavily armed, and fighting was to break out over a wide area of southeast O'ahu.

By a further coincidence, one hundred Japanese workers marched from Kahuku Plantation, on the northern point of the island, toward the port of Honolulu, aggrieved by their living and working conditions. The port newspaper, *The Friend,* reported that police squads met the strikers and marched them to jail.[3] In a less than friendly vein, *The Friend* reported that the strike had spread from the windward side of the island to the leeward side. Following the initial arrests, "300 Japs start(ed) for the city from (leeward) Ewa Plantation, with the grievance that police have interfered with their gathering." Japanese officials, likely from the Japanese consulate, turned the striking workers back, "thus saving the Government trouble in a time of terrible peril."

One may imagine that rumors of unrest in Honolulu swirled

around the aging Marujiro, first in the hold of the S.S. *Bentala* and then in the detainment area of the Customs House. Not only were the Hawaiians rising up against the white provisional government, but, the planters feared, perhaps the Japanese workers were rebelling as well.

When things cooled down, *The Friend* admitted there was no connection between the two events. For reassurance as to its moral high ground, *The Friend* turned to a Japanese minister of the Congregational Church, the Reverend Jiro Okabe, who swore allegiance to the Republic of Hawai'i as a means of reducing the tensions surrounding the plantation workers and also the workers-to-be in the port.

Standard histories were to portray Asians as bystanders in the saga of overthrow and annexation. This was not entirely accurate. The Chinese had lived in Hawai'i for half a century, and a large group petitioned for the right to vote in what was the interim provisional government. They were ignored. A group of Japanese likewise petitioned for the right to vote, and they too were ignored. Most Native Hawaiian voters likewise were disenfranchised, by income or property requirements, as African Americans had been disenfranchised in the American south, so that the Republic of Hawai'i had become, in the words of one sarcastic observer, a country without a citizenship.

Despite its involvement in the overthrow, America declined to immediately annex Hawai'i, as the sugar planters had hoped, but did provide *de facto* cover for the insurrectionists by stationing warships in Honolulu Harbor. Japan was alarmed. Were its emigrants being well treated? The year of Marujiro's arrival in Honolulu, Japan anchored its own man-o'-war in the harbor, announcing what turned out to be its temporary opposition to the annexation.

What a strange scene this must have been for Marujiro. Warships and guns were framed by the tranquil mountain peaks, afloat in billowing clouds. Two hundred rebellious Hawaiians replaced the one hundred striking Japanese in the jail. And it was in this context that Marujiro and his hundreds of shipmates were let through the Customs House for redistribution to the plantations of O'ahu, Kaua'i, Maui, Moloka'i, and Hawai'i Island.

Assignments to the plantations customarily took a few days, during which time the new arrivals might wander through Honolulu, sleeping over at a Japanese boarding house near the harbor, typically paying forty cents or so for a bed and ten to fifteen cents for a Japanese meal.

Marujiro was sent to a plantation village called Pāpa'ikou north of Hilo on the island of Hawai'i, where he went to work for fifteen dollars a month. Laborers at Pāpaʻikou worked ten hours a day, six days a week. Where Pāpaʻikou was situated, the sun beat down in summer as if this were Japan, and in winter the wind blew up cold rains that continued for weeks. A sick employee might be required to work unless he had a doctor's certificate, but there were no doctors on the scene to write certificates. On occasion an overseer, whip in hand, would roust a worker from his sickbed to labor in the field.

For such reasons, Japanese were jumping their contracts by the hundreds—a reported three hundred seventy-five in a single year. In this regard, they were not the docile people that the white planters had imagined. The agents of the plantations sought to chase the workers down, aided by the government and also by the Japanese immigration companies, which posted bonds as guarantees of a worker's faithful performance. Accordingly, although a contract worker was not quite a slave, neither was he quite free. Recaptured runaways were either jailed or returned to their respective plantations.

It was against this background that the next step in the Miwa family story was to occur. Two years after Marujiro's arrival, his oldest son, Senkichi Miwa, appeared in Hawai'i. While conceivably Senkichi had his own problems and needed a place to go, more likely Marujiro needed a substitute to fulfill his three-year labor contract. This would allow him to return home without becoming a fugitive. Marujiro's aging body may have been breaking down under the workload, but age also had its rewards. The health of his father-in-law was declining, and the Miwas of Hiroshima Prefecture needed a new headman.

Marujiro became one of a large number of immigrant workers about whom little is known—the roughly one-third who opted to return to Japan, as planned. Fatefully, he set a precedent for the Miwas that was to be enacted over and over—the precedent of the two-way journey. On June 12, 1900, according to the Furuichi Village register, Marujiro became the head of the Miwa clan, a role for which he had long waited.

Marujiro lived another nineteen years, to the age of sixty-nine. In his lifetime, the partially formed Japan of his birth had disappeared into mythology, a legendary land of courtliness and poetry. It had been replaced by a society that aspired to be a great nation in twentieth-century terms. He had survived his fall from the prescribed status of the samurai. He had fathered a large family. He had witnessed the coastal town of Hiroshima grow into a city. He lived out his years in an atmosphere of ever-accelerating change, of which his children became temporary beneficiaries, his oldest son Senkichi most of all.

CHAPTER TWO
The Merchant's Story

Senkichi Miwa was born on August 9, 1871. Four brothers and three sisters followed. In the year of Senkichi's birth, Japan began to organize a national army. When Senkichi was an infant, Japan instituted universal military service. As he started school, the nation began to require that students participate in military drills daily.

As Senkichi grew to adulthood, Hiroshima became the headquarters of Japan's Fifth Army Division, increasingly the scene of firing ranges, armories, parade fields, and barracks. More visibly than most places in Japan, Hiroshima was moving to a war footing. The main national rail line welded Hiroshima to the industrializing cities of eastern Japan, facing the Pacific. Hiroshima's natural harbor was developed as a port. These two essential features, the rail line and the port, were connected in 1894 by a spur line. This was accomplished in a two-week burst of frenetic work brought on by Japan's first industrialized war, which was with China. From throughout Japan, troops and war matériel were shipped to Hiroshima by rail, then transshipped by the spur line to the port, and then shipped by sea into the war zone.

With Hiroshima's strategic location, its natural advantages, and its new public works, it became Japan's crucial staging area for the military mobilization of 1894–1895. The national government temporarily moved to Hiroshima, and the emperor himself lived in Hiroshima Castle during part of the autumn, the winter, and the following spring. As a result of its natural assets and its important role in the rapidly rising nation-state, Hiroshima prospered.

Senkichi was twenty-three when the war with China began. As his father Marujiro was departing for Hawai'i, Senkichi temporarily became a soldier in Japan. Almost certainly he would have served with the Fifth Army Division. From an imperial viewpoint, the war was a great success. Japan gained the upper hand over China and became the dominant power of Korea, and then Korea's colonizer.

Senkichi was not a child of privilege but, to his eventual benefit, education in Meiji Japan had become mandatory up to the sixth grade, followed by at least part-time education for two years. Otherwise he lacked assets. He likely was demobilized from soldiering with no income and no means of support. He married a woman named Sata Furukawa who was several months pregnant. Judging by the tenacity with which he maintained his relationship with the child, a boy, he was the biological father. They named the baby Seigo Miwa, who was later to become widely known in Honolulu as James Seigo Miwa, the father of Lawrence Fumio Miwa, Stephen's father.

Senkichi left his new wife and son behind and emigrated to the Big Island of Hawaiʻi. In early 1897, he traded places with Marujiro. When Marujiro went home to claim his family role, Senkichi stayed on. He worked for Papaikou Plantation briefly, then looked around Hawaiʻi for opportunities of personal advancement. The census of 1900 was the first census in the new U.S. Territory of Hawaiʻi. It identified Senkichi Miwa as being twenty-nine years old, and as living in a boarding house in the town of Hilo. He was listed as a laborer who neither read nor wrote—that is, he did not read and write English. Nor did he speak English, in the view of the census taker. Nor did he speak Hawaiian. He boarded with a Japanese couple and their daughter, along with two other boarders. One boarder was listed as a laborer, the second as a clerk.

One explanation for this arrangement, which was fairly common to Hilo, was that Senkichi's landlord was a tenant sugar farmer, and that Senkichi had found work with him after fulfilling Marujiro's work agreement. If so, the tenant farmer provided a role model of a sort. He was no longer a wage worker but rather had achieved a modest measure of independence from the plantations. Senkichi's other fellow boarder, the clerk, likewise might have served as an inspiration of a sort for negotiating the barriers of language and culture.

In 1901, Senkichi left Hawaiʻi Island for Hiroshima. There he divorced Sata, whose name was stricken from the Miwa family line of the village registry in Furuichi, and married a second woman from Furuichi named Kiyo. For those who cherish the image of Japanese families joined solidly in place by arranged marriages, Senkichi's marital record may come as a surprise, as might those of his siblings. Senkichi's oldest sister, Hana, was married in 1892 and divorced sometime thereafter. In 1901 she married a man who claimed paternity of her two daughters. Senkichi's next oldest brother was married and divorced no fewer than six times. His third brother was married and divorced, as was his second sister.

The adoption tradition in their family—traceable to Marujiro—continued into Senkichi's generation, to no one's apparent satisfaction. In the second son's third marriage, he was adopted by his in-laws. His name was stricken from the Miwa line in the village record according to custom. On divorce, he was reinstated. Likewise, the fourth son was adopted by his wife's family, only to depart from and then return to the Miwa register as a result of divorce. Perhaps the arranging of marriages kept Marujiro and his wife busy into old age—assuming they did not abandon tradition out of emotional fatigue.

As Hawai'i was pulled into the world power system, the excitement of war or the threat of war often affected the atmosphere. When word of Japan's 1895 victory over China arrived, the Japanese consulate in Honolulu put up a twenty-foot-high arch, decorated by flags and flowers, topped by a sign that said "Emperor, Banzai."[1] The Japanese community staged a mock military parade around the city, led by a marching band. The accompanying ceremony was punctuated by 101 rounds of cannon fire.

In Senkichi's second year in Hawai'i, 1898, war erupted between the United States and Spain. It began not in Cuba, as the most iconic images were to suggest, but in Manila Harbor in the Philippines, where the U.S. Navy sank the decrepit Spanish fleet. Thereafter shiploads of American soldiers steamed into the Pacific to provide cover for the U.S. Navy, stopping to refuel coal in Honolulu. A committee of one hundred white citizens of the Republic of Hawai'i sailed out past Diamond Head to greet the American soldiers, escorting them to a *lū'au* on the grounds of 'Iolani Palace. It was shortly thereafter that the U.S. government, in a war fever, took over direct control of Hawai'i. As a result, Senkichi Miwa became a resident alien of the Territory of Hawai'i, which gave him legal standing in the United States.

Turmoil in the Pacific continued, driven by the aggressive behavior of both the United States and Japan. The United States waged a long-term war against the Filipinos to maintain control of the Philippines. In 1904, Japan launched a surprise attack against Russia's forces at a place called Port Arthur on a peninsula of beleaguered northern China.

As an overseas citizen of Japan, Senkichi was called to return to the homeland and serve a second time in the Japanese army. In this, Japan's second modern war, three of his brothers served as well. Senkichi apparently served close to home, perhaps in Hiroshima itself, because in May 1905, a week after Japan had defeated Russia, Senkichi sailed back to Honolulu in the company of his wife Kiyo.

Notes in the ship logs reflect the tensions in Hawai'i resulting from the transition from native control of the Hawaiian kingdom to U.S. control of the Territory of Hawai'i. Following a practice started by the interim Republic of Hawai'i, the U.S. Customs House asked the returning Senkichi if he had fifty dollars on his person. Nineteen dollars, Senkichi replied.

Was he entering the United States "by reason of any offer, solicitation, promise, or agreement, express or implied, to labor in the United States?" No.

Had he ever been in prison or in an almshouse? Was he a polygamist? An anarchist? A cripple? No, no, no, and no.

A shipboard doctor scrawled across the log, "These Japanese are found to be free of loathsome and contagious disease."

These were challenging years for Senkichi. Larry Miwa grew up with a clear impression that his grandfather struggled against the odds in this first decade of the twentieth century. It was, he said, a period of "hardship, failures, suffering, and starting over." For all that was ever known, Senkichi's service in the 1905 war might well have required him to give up either a job or business opportunities.

Opportunity in Hawai'i was elusive. The relatively welcoming entry to plantation Hawai'i decidedly did not extend to the United States as a country. Naturalization to U.S. citizenship was prohibited. With Hawai'i in American hands, the white oligarchy consolidated its position through interlocking corporations, the Big Five, as they were called, as well as the Republican Party. The Big Five controlled vast sectors of the economy and did not welcome competition—all in all, forming a tight little group of wealth and power. To advance, Japanese who left the plantation were relegated to searching out niches that largely resulted from the presence of a large number of their fellow immigrants.

By 1907, Japan and the United States were so at odds as to generate talk of war. Senkichi nonetheless was determined to become a businessman. He traveled the Pacific often. Less than a year after the war, he went back to Japan, then quickly returned to Honolulu. According to a Japanese *Who's Who in Business*, Senkichi then departed for San Francisco and worked several years for what was described as a white firm. By 1910 he was back in Hilo, working for the Hilo Wine and Liquor Company.

Senkichi moved from Hilo to Honolulu in 1911. That year he crossed the crucial threshold from employment by others to self-employment. He opened a store selling "Hay, Feed and Grain," in the words of his City Directory listing. He specialized in horse feed.

The storefront was substantial, sixty or so feet wide. It was located on a lateral thoroughfare at 1130 North King Street, just far enough from Honolulu's Chinatown to be at the edge of the city. It sat next to Kapālama Stream, which in heavy rains would flood the store. Whenever this happened, Senkichi sold the damaged goods at drastically lowered prices and regrouped.

He lived behind the store with his new wife Kiyo, who came to be regarded as severe in her personal dealings but sharp in business—a force in the background of Senkichi.

In 1911, Miwa Store was one of sixteen stores advertised in the business of Hay, Feed and Grain. The California Feed Company, five blocks toward downtown, was doing so well that it could afford a display advertisement on the cover of the City Directory. This put it in a league with the downtown Alexander Hotel, the Moana Hotel in Waikīkī, and the banks, all of which were owned by the overlapping business interests of the Big Five.

Miwa's fellow Hay, Feed and Grain dealers were listed alphabetically, some with generic business names but three with Chinese names: Wing On, Kwong Loy, and Man On Chan. Only Senkichi Miwa was Japanese.

Having survived the perils of startup, Senkichi began to chart a more ambitious future. The number of competitors in his business niche fell from fifteen to ten. California Feed took over a two-story building downtown, five companies now had Chinese names, and a second Japanese company entered the market.

That year, 1914, Senkichi sent for Seigo, son of the divorced Sata, with whom he had maintained an off-and-on contact. Seigo was by then seventeen years old.

A mere decade after Senkichi told a steamship purser that he had nineteen dollars in his pocket, he sailed to Japan in first class. Bigger things were in the making. He turned around to Honolulu quickly, then sailed to San Francisco to set up another store—his first step toward creating a truly trans-Pacific business.

Although Japanese in Hawai'i were still treated during this period as outsiders, they were becoming entrenched in niche businesses in the life of haole-dominated Hawai'i. Foremost was the fact that Japanese business catered to a large population of ethnic Japanese who had distinctive tastes. Japanese immigrants, most of whom came to work on the plantations, provided the basis for Japanese business. By the hundreds at a time, Japanese arrived on ships with Japanese names, such as the *City of Tokyo,* the *Yamashiro Maru,* the *Omi Maru,* and the *Sagami Maru.* They stayed at Japanese hotels, ate at Japanese restaurants, and drank at Japanese bars. This was a luxury of ethnocentric habits resulting from a large migration—thirty thousand Japanese in the first decade beginning in 1885; another fifty-seven thousand in the next years (1894–1900, the time window of Marujiro and Senkichi); and over seventy thousand in the first seven years of the American period (1900–1907).

During this early period of Japanese migration, most of the immigrants were male. Single men, after lonely lives, were buried in stark plantation graveyards, which dotted the landscape far and wide. More Japanese died than were born.

In 1907, an international crisis occurred between Japan and the United States over the treatment of Japanese on the West Coast, most of whom had moved on from Hawai'i—or transmigrated—in search of higher wages or farmland. The threat of war was averted by a secret Gentleman's Agreement, as it was to be called, virtually shutting down migration into the West Coast but allowing prospective Japanese wives into the Territory of Hawai'i. Usually the match was made by an exchange of photographs—hence the legend of the picture bride. Between the Gentleman's Agreement of 1907 and the near-complete close of Japanese immigration in 1924, sixty-one thousand Japanese were added to the thriving community of Hawai'i. Because most were female, instantly married, the effect was to accelerate the population explosion. The net negative mortality rate was dramatically reversed.

Live births soon outnumbered deaths by a ratio of five to one. Young Americans of Japanese ancestry were ubiquitous. With a certain anxiety on the part of non-Japanese, it would often be noted that the ethnically Japanese made up nearly forty percent of the Territory of Hawai'i's people.

Having located the opportunity of such a robust market, Senkichi also had a problem. Much of his business revolved around horses. A photograph taken of the Miwa establishment showed horse and buggy rigs lining the property from end to end, primed to deliver orders to the customers, who themselves were primarily horse owners. However, the first two automobiles had arrived in Honolulu in 1899, and use of the car naturally increased year after year, which meant that Senkichi had to do something about his business model.

Simultaneously, a succession of international events influenced the Hawaiian economy. In the lead-up to World War I, Britain formed an alliance in the Pacific with Japan. In fulfillment of their end of the bargain, Japan's navy chased a number of enemy German ships into Honolulu Harbor. They then lay offshore, trapped one German schooner, and torched it. They tied up another for the duration, an "internment," as it was called. Belatedly, the Anglo-Japanese alliance of convenience in World War I extended to America. For the moment, all was well in the relationship between Japan and the United States.

Senkichi still crossed the Pacific frequently, using this period to update and expand his business. The Hiroshima *Who's Who* said he began importing goods from Japan into Hawai'i in 1917, the year of America's entry into the war. In the Honolulu City Directory of 1920, the words "flour" and "Japan rice" were added to the words "hay, grain and feed." Now Senkichi was in the food importing business, as well as the farm-support business. To people who could not afford a car, Senkichi was delivering groceries in a timely way. In his next storefront photo, the horses were gone, replaced by a large fleet of Model T Fords and small trucks, their drivers at the ready.

In this same brief time frame, the hereditary system of the Miwa clan of Furuichi Village came knocking. Primogeniture reigned. At age forty-seven, in August 1918, Senkichi became head of the family, replacing the samurai Marujiro. Despite modernization, Japan's steadfast attachment to the prerogatives and responsibilities of the oldest son had survived. Marujiro died the next year, and his remains were placed in the Miwa family plot above the now rapidly growing city of Hiroshima. Just as leadership of the Miwa clan had taken Marujiro back to Japan, Senkichi was now determined to go back to Japan as well, but first he had to position a successor in Honolulu.

IN THE MEANTIME, JAMES SEIGO MIWA had graduated from high school and joined Senkichi in business. Despite his youth and limited experience, he rose quickly to a position of leadership.

During this period Senkichi also sent out a call to his youngest brother, Kanroku, who had been working in a fish cannery in Anchorage, Alaska. Kanroku and his family moved to Honolulu, and began living and working at the North King Street store. On the side, Kanroku distilled *sake* from the store's rice supplies and drank considerably, according to an account left by a son, Ralph Miwa, who was, in reaction, a teetotaler. Kanroku eventually returned to Hiroshima, where he was to die at age fifty in 1941.

Senkichi Miwa and his son James Seigo Miwa were both not only capable but ambitious. The coming phase of their business development required a higher level of finesse. It challenged them to thread their way in tandem through the white-dominated business climate of Hawai'i, as well as the increasingly militarized Hiroshima. With James Seigo pulling a heavy workload in Honolulu, Senkichi relocated to Hiroshima. He continued his travels back and forth, but from then on, his main focus was Hiroshima.

In all of this, Senkichi demonstrated considerable powers of intelligence, determination, and adaptation. He now was deep into middle age, but it seemed he was just getting started, while young James Seigo was as yet an unknown quantity.

PART II

Between

CHAPTER THREE
Turning a Profit

The great expanse of ocean separating Japan and Hawai'i was emblematic of James Seigo Miwa, in that he would always reflect a division within himself.

From the perspective of Japan, the value and meaning of Hawai'i were subject to change. Hawai'i was no longer an independent Polynesian kingdom, as it had been in the experience of Marujiro and Senkichi, but an overseas territory of the United States. Where the Japan of James Seigo's early childhood tended to idealize modernity and the West, Japan regained a stronger sense of identity as it succeeded on the world stage. Outmigration from Japan, once fervently supported, became a source of frustration for the Japanese government and sometimes a source of humiliation. As America's pattern of racial discrimination became apparent, Japan shifted its focus from Hawai'i to Brazil.[1]

James Seigo's personal status as a child of divorce was similarly uncertain. As a number one son, he was potentially privileged. However, he initially was under the primary care of his mother, Sata Furukawa, and Senkichi was a long-distance father. Although Senkichi sent money, he appeared only occasionally in the flesh. Sata would have been sharply aware that Senkichi's new wife might give birth to a competing heir, but as years passed Senkichi and Kiyo remained childless. Year by year, Seigo emerged as the sole and therefore indispensable offspring.

Senkichi summoned him to Hawai'i in 1914. He departed Japan as Seigo Miwa and after a short while in Hawai'i he became known as James Miwa. Leaving Sata behind, he was the one hundred and first passenger, and also the last, crammed into the hull of a ship called the S.S. *Manchuria*. Even the ship's name was clutched by history, derived as it was from the land beyond Korea that Japan coveted.

Where Senkichi had a pinched look, James was bigger and more rugged. He was five feet, eight inches tall, of medium build. By most accounts, he was more outgoing than his father. His shipmates included other Japanese—an Okano, a Yamashita, a Saiki, a Hirota, and a Sunahara. Although the ship's last port of call was the coast of China, none of the passengers was Chinese, who at that point had been prohibited altogether from entering the United States or its territories by the 1882 Chinese Exclusion Act.

The crossing took eleven days.

In the brief span of two decades, James was the third generation of Miwas to migrate to Hawai'i. But because James had not been born on U.S. soil, he was a Japanese alien ineligible for American citizenship under U.S. law.

He was now in the domain of his stepmother Kiyo—she of the sharp tongue—and they quickly conflicted. He was sent across town to a missionary-inspired boarding school, Mills Institute, which was soon to be renamed Mid-Pacific Institute.

The school lay in the middle of Mānoa Valley, surrounded on three sides by creviced mountain ridges and on the downhill side by the University of Hawai'i and Punahou School. Set on generous green lawns, Mills Institute's landmark was a four-story multi-purpose building of dark brown native stone. The school dated its history to 1864, when a Christian missionary opened the doors of his home to eight Native Hawaiian boarding students. In the early 1890s a second missionary opened his home to a group of Chinese students. Mills resulted from combining the two home-based boarding schools. It soon added many Japanese students, reflecting the large number of arriving Japanese.

Nearly a century after the original wave of American missionaries, Mills Institute continued to function as an internationally oriented extension of the missionary tradition. In that sense, Mills was a testimony to the dedication of the missionaries. The two most influential board members were Theodore Richards and Frank Atherton. Richards was a Pacific bridge builder, particularly of ties between Hawai'i and Japan. Atherton was a major mover behind organizations with suggestive names such as Hands Around the Pacific, the Pan-Pacific Union, and the Institute for Pacific Relations. All shared a hope for an open, prosperous Pacific, notwithstanding the recurring tensions between Japan and America.

James was assigned to the seventh grade. To be seventeen years old and a seventh grader was less embarrassing than it may sound, because the school often took in students who spoke virtually no English. At the extreme, Mills would enroll a nearly grown man in the first or second grade, advancing him whenever he was deemed ready.

Students were awakened at Mills at 6 a.m. They did chores and then ate breakfast at 7:00. Each student then stood inspection by his bed. Classes began at 8 a.m. and ran to 1 p.m. Students on work scholarship turned to their jobs. If they were not working, students were required to participate in sports. The nearly all-white faculty and their nearly all-Asian students together built their own tennis court, which was the root of the Miwa tennis tradition that Lawrence, Stephen, and Stephen's daughter were to perpetuate.

Dinner was at 6:00, followed by a two-hour study hall. Lights went out at 9:30. The work continued into noon on Saturday, and attendance at a Christian Sunday church was mandatory.

Instruction in the early grades included mechanics and agriculture. The school had its own farm, providing it with a degree of food sufficiency. From the eighth grade on, the curriculum provided a course in commerce. Influenced by a desire to compete with Punahou School and McKinley High School, Mills added a class on the Roman orator Cicero, as well as classes in Latin.

The many Asian students were not merely tolerated but embraced, provided they attended Bible study twice a week and took their Christian teachings seriously. It was at the point he converted to Christianity and was baptized that Seigo became James. From then on, throughout all of his life, he would alternate between his new Western name and his Japanese name.

James wanted to be a doctor. Senkichi told him if he finished first in his class, he would send him to medical school. James made high marks, despite the limitations of his English, but finished third. Obviously Senkichi had other plans for him. The energy that James might have given to doctoring and healing, he now poured into learning the feed, grain, and food import business. His period of on-the-job training was to last only two years, at which point the departing Senkichi put James in charge.

ACCORDING TO HAWAI‘I'S JAPANESE WHO'S WHO, Senkichi made his move in 1921. From Japan, he set up supply lines for expanding the export of Japanese goods to Hawai‘i, including rice, which immigrant Japanese consumers deemed to be special. The Who's Who reported that Senkichi set up his own separate trading company. During this transition, he made several more trips back and forth between Hawai'i and Japan.

Thereafter Senkichi and his wife Kiyo would occasionally drop in to Hawai'i, and as late as 1927 he was identified along with James as a prominent Hawai'i businessman. Otherwise, Senkichi receded in visibility in Honolulu while James rose to a prominence that would considerably outdo his father's.

The *Who's Who* described James as "steady but keen in finding business opportunities," an acknowledgment of his ability to expand. Further, "he [was] the man of surprise and respect from the senior merchants." He upgraded the old wooden headquarters building on King Street with a new, modern concrete façade and bold contemporary lettering proclaiming the J. S. MIWA BLDG. He opened a second store just above downtown, in Nu'uanu, and a third store in Mō'ili'ili, a heavily Japanese neighborhood in the plains of lower Mānoa Valley below the University of Hawai'i.

New stationery identified him as an importer and exporter with offices in Honolulu, Hiroshima, and San Francisco. He was pan-Pacific, a term whose increasingly extensive use reflected its being a widely held goal of the time. James used the Japanese word *Shoten* for store, and *Shokai* for trading company. The stores were neighborhood retail

James Seigo Miwa, son of Senkichi Miwa, grandson of Miwa Marujiro. (Miwa Family Collection)

J. S. Miwa letterhead reflecting Japan, Honolulu, and San Francisco addresses. (Miwa Family Collection)

stores, while the J. S. Miwa store on King Street was more of a warehouse operation. It was considerably larger and more dynamic in its potential as a wholesale/retail business that supplied, among others, the small farmer.

On James's new stationery, the Japanese word *Marusan* would turn out to be too Japanese and therefore a mistake vis-à-vis the gathering cloud of American internal security. It was part of the name *Marusan Shokai,* referring to the trading company that Senkichi had organized when he returned to Yokogawa. The second use of the word *Marusan* referred to Senkichi's rubber manufacturing company in Hiroshima, the Marusan Rubber Company.

James regularly sent money to his father. James's son Lawrence came to believe this was a matter of James buying the stores from Senkichi incrementally, but possibly the two had a more partnering type of business relationship. James was undoubtedly in an expansion mode, and Senkichi—despite his advancing age—likewise displayed an entrepreneurial spirit. At any rate, the net effect was that the business in Hawai'i helped finance valuable new enterprises in Yokogawa.

The Yokogawa address on James's letterhead, 655 *Miwamachi-chome* (Miwa Town Street) was the address of the family compound.

An early version of the Miwa storefront in Kalihi, Oʻahu, circa 1915. (Bishop Museum Archives)

A modernized version of the Miwas' main store, reflecting the influence of James Seigo Miwa, 1932. (Miwa Family Collection)

The Marusan Rubber Company was located nearby, as was Senkichi's most unusual indulgence, a horse racing track, where his own horse was stabled.

Wedged among all these events was the question of whether James would marry and, if so, where and in what tradition. In what must have been a stormy drama, James married not once but twice, both times in Hiroshima. In a period of thirty-six days, at age twenty-three, he married and divorced Matsuko Sakamoto, then married Yoshio Takeda. Why is unclear.

Yoshio was to endure. She was the youngest of three daughters. Perhaps she had developed an inner strength by fending off the dominating behavior of older siblings, as she would prove to be a bright and strong figure in the family story.

James and Yoshio's first child, a girl, Kiyoko, was born in Hawai'i two years later, in 1923. Kiyoko was to become Stephen's informant, Aunt Katherine. She was also the first of the fourth generation of the migrating Miwas. A boy, Shozo, was born in 1926, three years later. Another male child was born in 1929 but lived only three weeks. The youngest son, Lawrence Fumio, was born in 1931, with the result that eight years separated the three children.

The births of the three surviving children coincided with a downward spiral of action and reaction between Japan and the United States. In 1924, the U.S. Congress passed the first wholly race-based immigration act, popularly referred to as the Japanese Exclusion Act. In a phrase originating in California, this was an attempt to maintain the United States as "a white man's country."

Up to this point, there had been an ongoing competition within Japan between merchants wanting to do business with the West on the one hand versus militarists on the other. In these terms, the Miwas would have been at least vaguely aligned with the merchant viewpoint. In many accountings of Japan's history, the insult of the Japanese Exclusion Act tipped the scales. Virtually unnoticed by the U.S. citizenry, the streets of Tokyo filled with angry protestors. Militarists gained the upper hand in Japanese politics, and the idea of working in an international system with America and Europe gave way to visions of an Asian and Pacific Island empire. In 1925 Japan adopted what was euphemistically referred to as the Peace Preservation Law, creating a "thought police" that arrested people by the thousands for anything that smacked of anti-government criticism.

In 1931, the year of Larry Miwa's birth, Japan's field army—the famous Kwantung Army—took it upon itself to blow up a Japanese rail line in Manchuria and to blame this act of apparent sabotage on China. Following this pivotal event, Japan's army set up the puppet state of Manchukuo, which up until then had been the northern reach of China. Japan's military had become answerable only to itself.

Despite such ominous events, it was as if the music played on for James Miwa. He emerged as a bright young member of Honolulu's Japanese business community. He took up golf. He became one of sixty-six members of the Japanese Chamber of Commerce, which met in Honolulu's Japanese teahouses, of which there were several dozen at the time. Many of the members of the Japanese Chamber were from Hiroshima, and some had attended Mid-Pacific (formerly Mills) Institute. Everyone was interested in business. A few, like James, moved back and forth, doing business in two worlds, but the norm was for a Japanese business to take root in Hawai'i.

Where Senkichi had left off his habit of traversing the Pacific, James took it up. In 1925, he went to San Francisco. In 1926, he went to Japan. The next year he again went to San Francisco. This travel pattern continued, usually with one or two trips a year.

As his family grew, he moved them to Kapahulu, near the Ala Wai golf course, which is next to Waikīkī. From there they moved to a house behind the store in Mō'ili'ili, a community in which Japanese were a considerable presence. One short block held the Mō'ili'ili Japanese Language School, the Hatanaka Stone Factory, Nekota Store, Yamada Barber Shop, Suehiro Watch Store, and Watanabe Store. Just beyond were Japanese taxi stands, jewelry shops, auto body shops, *okazu-ya* (delicatessens), a Japanese bakery, a Japanese fish cutter, a Japanese plumber, a Japanese laundry, a Japanese pharmacy, and a tofu shop, each of them testimony to hard work, enterprise, and a large customer base of Japanese.

The year of Larry's birth, James was elected to the board of directors of the Japanese Chamber of Commerce, which was just down the street. Over the next sixteen years, he would be variously listed in Japanese Chamber publications as a director, councilor, auditor, and subcommittee member on trade and wholesale.

In 1933, James and his wife Yoshio relocated Katherine to the family compound in Hiroshima. Katherine was nine. The next year they relocated Shozo, seven. The following year, Yoshio took two-year-old Lawrence Fumio to Japan.

The entire family was now regrouped in Japan except for James, who continued to move back and forth, conducting business in Hawai'i and San Francisco as well as Hiroshima. Katherine, Shozo, and Lawrence were all American citizens by birth, but they were also dual citizens, and now they were being educated and trained in the language and culture of Japan.

The Hiroshima of this period was becoming ever more dominated by the Japanese Army, including a variety of factories that supported the war effort. From mid-1935 to the late spring of 1936, for nearly ten months, James again visited Japan. Thereafter he no sooner had returned to Hawai'i than he again traveled to Japan—this, in an apparent attempt to keep his resident visa current.

James was to tell American investigators he traveled so much because of Senkichi's declining health. At this point, Senkichi lived in his synthesized Japanese- and American-style house with his wife Kiyo and his aged mother. James's wife and children lived part of the time in Osaka, where the Miwas did business, and then they lived near Senkichi, but separately.

As the children grew, Grandfather Senkichi loomed large in their perceptions. He was the "big man" whose memory still lived on in the streets of Yokogawa into the twenty-first century. The Meiji Era had opened the country to migration, and first Marujiro and then he had been free to migrate to Hawai'i. He had evolved from a plantation worker to store clerk to store owner. He had become wealthy. He crossed the Pacific numerous times during a period when most people never left their home village. As a developer, he had not only cut the road called Miwa Street but lined it with rental houses and rental shops. He owned a stable and a racetrack.

Stephen's one surviving photograph of Senkichi seemed to tell the story of his life's diversity. He sat astride his fine horse on Miwa Street, outside his imposing bicultural house, which peeked from behind a high wall. He was seated on a pancake English saddle, dressed in a pith helmet, a blazer, and knee-high leather boots. Given that the average height of an adult Japanese male was five feet and two inches, he may have been of average height. He died in 1937 at the age of sixty-six.

JAMES GAVE HIM A FUNERAL BEFITTING a person of high status. A long column of hired mourners, dressed in costumes from the samurai era, paraded down Miwa Street. The mourners, numbering a hundred and fifty to two hundred, walked together to a temple, a half hour away, where the family collected Senkichi's cremated ashes, which then were placed in the family grave in the mountain village of Furuichi.

The event culminated in an explosive confrontation between James and Senkichi's wife, the newly widowed Kiyo. What was said between son and stepmother went unrecorded, but what happened did not. The two quarreled openly in Katherine's presence. The widow

Senkichi Miwa, son of the samurai Marujiro, father of James Seigo Miwa, astride his steed in front of the bicultural family compound on Miwa Street in the Yokogawa District of Hiroshima, mid-1930s. (Miwa Family Collection)

Kiyo well might have done what a woman of the time was expected to do, which was to keep her mouth shut. Instead she engaged James in an argument. She then slapped him, the oldest and only son of the deceased, across the face. Following The Slap, as it came to be called, Kiyo was moved out of the Miwa compound into a Miwa rental property, and James Miwa's immediate family—his wife Yoshio, his daughter Katherine, and his sons Shozo and Lawrence Fumio—moved into the culturally bifurcated big house.

The children became privileged members of the Yokogawa neighborhood, sheltered by the Miwa compound yet free to explore the playgrounds, parks, and schools of the area. Their domain ranged from the rail line, down Miwa Street, and across the Yokogawa Bridge, to the Hiroshima Prefectural Industrial Promotion Hall that, along with the Hiroshima Castle, was a proud symbol of the thriving Hiroshima.

James was likely at the height of his influence in business. After Senkichi's death, he walked his son Lawrence Fumio, then seven, through the Marusan Rubber Factory. Lawrence would recall the workforce as being fifty to one hundred people, almost all women. To his

James Seigo Miwa and his wife Yoshio, photographed in the 1930s, in front of
the Itsukushima Shrine on Miyajima Island in Hiroshima Bay. (Miwa Family
Collection)

knowledge, the factory produced commercial rubber products and not
products for military use.

The issues posed by Senkichi's death threw James off of his travel
schedule, to his eventual detriment. He remained in Japan for more
than a year, from mid-August of 1937 to late November 1938. In the
process, he overstayed the terms of his passport, which meant that he
reentered the Territory of Hawai'i not on a long-term resident alien visa
but on a visitor visa. Worse, he now had a notation on his travel record
of interest to the Immigration and Naturalization Service of the United
States government.

The growing international tension notwithstanding, life in
Hawai'i remained consistently pleasant. James was better known in
Honolulu than in Hiroshima. He had influential friends and acquaintances across ethnic lines. He golfed more. Now in his early forties,
James was part of a small circle of people who shared the leadership of
the Japanese Chamber. The most dominant figures were businessmen
of the first generation. One was Kenkichi Iida, an importer of Japanese
household wares. The second was Daizo Sumida, a prominent executive

of a Japan-owned bank. The importer Iida and the banker Sumida traded off the Chamber presidency. Membership grew over a two-year period in the late 1930s from sixty-six to eighty-eight. The majority of the members were first-generation immigrants, or Issei, but twenty-five were of the second generation, the Nisei. Almost certainly James, as an alien, would have been counted among the Issei, even though now, because of the family's transnational lifestyle, he was the third generation of Miwas to live in the U.S. Territory of Hawai'i.

Japan was no longer so far away. People who had left Japan as young people on British and American ships now crossed the Pacific on Japanese steamers, as well as on the new diesel-powered liners. In 1938, international radiotelephone communication commenced between Tokyo and Honolulu. In the general election of the Territorial government of Hawai'i, a sizable handful of Japanese American candidates—nine in all—were elected to public offices. While they were few in numbers proportionate to the Japanese population, their success at the polls reflected political development, giving promise to the possibility that the Japanese community might one day establish a semblance of parity in elective office with the dominant whites.

James's most prestigious golfing partner was the acting consul general of the Japanese Consulate. His name was Binjiro Kudo. At the 1940 New Year's banquet of the Japanese Chamber, Kudo gave the congratulatory address. He was about to be reassigned from Honolulu to Canton, China (now Guangzhou), then recently invaded by Japan.

As an aspect of his farewell, Kudo wrote in the January 1940 issue of the quarterly *Pan Pacific* magazine of "the harmonious blending of the spirit of Aloha and goodwill [which] should prove a worthy contribution to the welfare, peace and happiness of mankind." His wife, as president of the Japanese Women's Society, wrote of getting acquainted with a wide range of women in Hawai'i. She ardently wished that "understanding and friendship" would make a lasting link between the two countries. "Undoubtedly," she said, "the Japanese women living in these islands also feel the same way as I do."

Their statements went beyond mere ritual. They vigorously affirmed the value of friendship with Americans and seized on the Aloha spirit as a metaphor for maintaining the peace. The Kudos' farewell was echoed by a tribute signed by a number of the most prominent citizens of Hawai'i, twenty-eight white citizens and eighteen persons of Japanese ancestry, many of whom were Americans.

Among the whites were the most influential executive of the Big Five corporations, Frank Atherton, as well as his in-law Theodore Richards, a vigorous and idealistic internationalist. Others included Ralph Cole, the president of the YMCA; Charles F. Loomis, the executive secretary of the Institute for Pacific Relations (IPR); Joseph Farrington, publisher of the afternoon *Honolulu Star-Bulletin,* which then was Hawai'i's largest newspaper; John A. Hamilton, the head of the Honolulu Chamber of Commerce; and the Reverend Galen R. Weaver, the pastor of a recently established and consciously multiracial Congregational church, the Church of the Crossroads. The list of Japanese Americans included a variety of budding entrepreneurs along with the distinguished attorney and Territorial legislator Wilfred C. Tsukiyama.

Relationships among them were substantially based in the internationalist YMCA and its offspring, the IPR, which quixotically attempted to promote a peaceful relationship between the United States and Japan in the midst of ever-accelerating preparations for war.

The Kudo family disappeared from Hawai'i, but they were to eventually reemerge in the life of the Miwas, providing Stephen Miwa with a mother who warned, "The Miwas are unlucky."

Around the time of the Kudos' departure, James Miwa gave a breezy interview to the Hawai'i-based Japanese language newspaper, the *Nippu Jiji,* in which he struck an admiring tone for Japan. At least as his remarks were interpreted by a Japanese reporter, he dismissed the idea that U.S. sanctions might hurt Japan's economy. "Japan," he said, "has already prepared against U.S. sanctions and it is rather the United States that will suffer the damage."

He suggested that people who were really interested in business expansion should look to Asia. "It's nice living comfortably in Hawai'i," he said, "but those ambitious people who want a challenge for their bright future should go out to Japan and even China." He said much had been made of Americans of Japanese ancestry (Nisei) who were doing business in the wider Hawai'i community. However, he ran on, dangerously for his future well-being, "It is in the best interest of the Japanese communities in Hawai'i to explore more business opportunities among themselves." In the context of the rapidly growing tension, his remarks as published could easily be read as a plug for an ethnic approach to business, as well as an approving word for Japan's invasion of China.

The article gingerly described him as being in his late thirties but said he looked younger because of sports. He was, in fact, forty-three. "I play golf for fun," he said, adding, "Thanks to golfing, I could get rid of my stubborn six-year-old asthma."

In an item of later interest to the U.S. government, the story identified him as president of Marusan Rubber Co. Ltd. in Hiroshima. If that were not sufficiently explicit, he was quoted several paragraphs later as saying, "I am now managing a rubber firm in Japan."[2] The article said further that Miwa held "the rare title" of Japanese government-contracted "Labor Researcher" for Japan and, as such, was related to the government of Japan at a high level, defined as the "Prime Minister's cabinet," which surely was an inflation of his status.[3]

Although James was increasingly active in terms of business travel, he was feeling the pressure of impending war. Nonetheless, he did nothing to distance himself from Japan or from the main figures in the Japanese immigrant community. He continued his activities with the Japanese Chamber of Commerce and in fact was elected to the Chamber's standing committee on commerce and appointed to its subcommittee on wholesale trade. His business was referred to in this context as Miwa *Shokai,* meaning it was a trading company linked directly to Japan.

At the end of January 1941, James sailed to San Francisco with his wife Yoshio. He stayed nearly six weeks, which was far longer than he usually did, presumably for a combination of pleasure and business. In a handwritten note, the ship's manifest described him and the other Japanese aliens on board as "Japs." Fear and loathing were intensifying on both sides.

He had been back in Hawai'i less than a week when he and Yoshio sailed for Japan, departing on April 1 for what would become for him a six-month stay in Hiroshima.

As a result of this six-month absence from Hawai'i, he skipped over a crucial period during which the future of the Japanese community was none too subtly being negotiated on the public stage. Cues were being passed back and forth as to what was expected of "the Japanese," as all were often lumped together, and what could be gained by their Americanization and fealty to the American nation in the event of war. A Council for Interracial Unity was at work, attempting to set the stage for maximizing Japanese American participation in the U.S. war effort, and thereby minimizing the pressure to arrest and incarcerate. The Nisei strategist for this effort, a young educator named Shigeo Yoshida, uttered a prophetic phrase that was to be repeated over and over: "How we get along during the war will determine how we get along when the war is over."

In midsummer, two thousand mostly Nisei students turned out for a patriotic rally at McKinley High School aimed at securing a continued place for themselves in the community in the event of war. In the key statement of the night, the head of U.S. Army Intelligence promised that if people obeyed the law and supported the war effort, they would be free to pursue their lives, work at their jobs, and reside in their own homes. It was an early attempt to take the idea of a mass internment in Hawai'i off the table.

The army commander, Lt. Gen. Walter C. Short, was asked by a Japanese weekly, *Jitsugyō no Hawaii,* to comment on the status of the Japanese community in the event of war. The medium was a special edition celebrating thirty years of continuous publication. Short said the Japanese problem was twofold: "First, they must assimilate the customs and spirit of Americanism with an unquestionable belief in and loyalty to the ideals of Americanism. Second, they must convince the community of Honolulu of their loyalty to Americanism and their profound belief in the ideals of Americanism." Were this not sufficiently pointed, he added, "The Japanese people in Hawaii are on probation." An attorney, Arthur D. Baldwin, with at least a passing understanding of Japanese literature, held up the *Forty-Seven Ronin* as a model for loyalty to America: "In old Japan the lord's retainers served him to the death," Baldwin wrote. "In the place of the old-time lord now stands their country, the United States of America. If they serve it with the same spirit which inspired their ancestors, there will be no question of the value of their citizenship to this country." This was a telling line. Japanese Americans were being urged by both their own community leaders and their own immigrant parents to devote an intensely Japanese version of "loyalty" to the nation of their birth.

Such statements filled the air of the midsummer and fall of 1941. Meanwhile, the FBI and the Honolulu Police Department were actively questioning and profiling thousands of people, mostly of Japanese ancestry, who were considered (in a vague phrase of internal security) "inimical to the interests of the United States."

All of this occurred while James was in Hiroshima. It was perhaps because of his absence that he failed to come to grips with the new reality: In the event of a war between Japan and the United States, there was to be no middle ground. Perpetually he had been a man in

The ship manifest noting James Seigo Miwa's arrival in Hawai'i (bottom line) reflects a standard treatment by U.S. Customs. (Ancestry.com)

the middle, owing to his transnational way of life and business, and the middle was giving way.

Meanwhile, he was a witness to life in Hiroshima, which was on an active, probably frantic, war footing. Japan's Fifth Army, home-based in Hiroshima, was deployed to China. Casualties and financial costs mounted. People had less food and less fuel. To prosecute the war, Japan needed oil and rubber. Its military plunged boldly into Southeast Asia to get them, but the allied Americans, British, and Dutch stood stubbornly in Japan's way.

In the midst of these developments, in early October 1941, James decided to leave his wife and three children behind in the compound on Miwa Street and return to Hawai'i. From Hiroshima he headed north, stopping on October 13 in the port of Kobe to pick up new travel papers. He then rushed on. His ship, the *Tatsuta Maru,* was nearly ready to sail from the familiar waters of Yokohama.[4]

The manifest of the *Tatsuta Maru* reflected a widespread apprehension of approaching war. It listed about five hundred fifty passengers

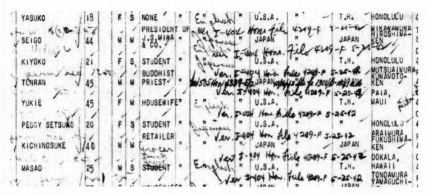

James Seigo Miwa's return to Hawai'i, October 23, 1941 (second line), reflects the anxiety of security agents as war approaches. (Ancestry.com)

of Japanese ancestry, many of them Japanese Americans who were clearing out of Japan. For example, loading onto the steamer along with James was a man from Hilo, Zenpachi Fujita, who said he was going to see his wife, Shizue. A young Japanese American woman was listed as "Geisha girl." Many were listed as students. Rose Yoshiko Hamada, ten, was being escorted home by her father, who worked for the Matson shipping lines in Hawai'i, and by her mother, a housewife. Seizuchi Kosa, sixty-five, was a mason. Only a few were plantation workers. Most had attained a niche in the growing economic sector of the Islands outside the direct control of the plantations. They had roots in Hawai'i and were urgently trying to return home.

In contrast to the great bulk of his fellow passengers, James was not clearly situated in either Japan or Hawai'i. Accordingly his way of life, which so often had made him travel back and forth, was deeply threatened. His family was in Japan, but a majority of his acquaintances and much of his material wealth were in Hawai'i.

The *Tatsuta Maru* was a grand ship of the NYK line, one of the biggest and fastest trans-Pacific liners afloat. It arrived in Honolulu on October 23, 1941. A raft of FBI agents, Federal Customs agents, and Honolulu police from its Espionage Unit descended on the ship. They studied the hundreds of passengers and pored over the notations on the ship's manifest. Distinguishing physical characteristics were noted. One person had a mole on the left cheek, another on the right cheek, another on the neck. One person had a small scar over the right eye, another over the left. Occasionally someone had a pockmark. In fact, almost everyone had a distinguishing mole, scar, or pockmark. One woman was examined by the ship's assistant surgeon, who filled out a special form for her. She was missing her right eye.

In the confusion, shipboard officers used two different forms for profiling passengers, where logically only one was needed. The more contemporary of the two forms asked a mere fifteen questions. The more archaic form, a vestige of the Republic of Hawai'i, asked thirty questions. In addition to asking if the passenger was an anarchist, it inquired whether he or she had fifty dollars in their pocket and, if not, how much. (This was a question with a dark history that had been contrived by the white oligarchy's five-year "Republic" to manipulate its nation-to-nation relationship with Japan. In 1897, fourteen hundred Japanese immigrants had been held in quarantine and then turned back as a way of heightening tensions with Japan, thereby creating an impetus for the American takeover of Hawai'i.)[5]

Where ship manifests were usually treated casually, all the check boxes on the *Tatsuta Maru* manifests were checked. Detailed questions, typically ignored in earlier voyages, were checked twice or even three times. Handwritten notes described the duration of visas and where those had been issued. In this regard, James was getting on progressively shakier ground. He previously had been in the United States on a trader visa, and now he returned on a visitor's permit, which was valid for only six months. It was not until the next day that the ship's surgeon signed off on the mass of paperwork that, at other times, had been abbreviated and treated as a matter of routine.[6]

THE SAME MONTH, OCTOBER 1941, THE Hawai'i Territorial Legislature in emergency session passed a bill, signed by the governor, suspending the constitutional rights of the resident public in the event of war. This was called the M-Day Bill, the "m" standing for mobilization, and was otherwise known as the Hawaiian Defense Act.

While the M-Day law was ominous on its face, within it lay James Miwa's opportunity to find a secure niche in the event of war. The law called for the creation of various committees to serve in war crisis at a policy level, including a Territorial Food Committee. For an alien such as James Miwa, the Food Committee was the front row of the entire community. The reason was that food supply was in approximately the same state of preparedness as the military defense, which is to say that surface appearance and underlying reality differed. Although O'ahu appeared to be a verdant garden, it was producing only a small fraction of its own food—by one widely quoted estimate, fifteen percent.

Prime agricultural land was devoted to producing sugar and pineapple, leaving independent farmers, typically Japanese, growing crops in small plots on marginally productive lands. If Oʻahu was to become more self-sufficient, it needed not only more fruits and vegetables but also more cows, sheep, pigs, chickens, and ducks, which in turn needed more of what James primarily dealt in, feed and grain.

The U.S. military had been raising the alarm over the food security of the Hawaiian Islands since the mid-1930s and, as the months of 1941 passed, the volume of the alarm rose. The addition of military personnel and civilian construction workers on the island meant there were more people to feed. At the same time, war-related matériel competed with foodstuffs for shipping space.

In the midsummer of 1941, the Science Association of Hawaiʻi urged the public to hoard food at home as a way of freeing shelf space to stock more food. General Short gave a food speech, recommending a federal appropriation of several million dollars to increase Hawaiʻi's food supply, including nearly a million dollars in feed for dairy cattle and poultry.

Against the specter of shortages, James seemed to be the right person at the right time in the right place. He knew in depth about something that urgently mattered under the circumstances, which was the myriad of ways that animal feed was sold and distributed to Oʻahu's small farmers.

ON NOVEMBER 26, 1941, THE ARMY, Navy, and FBI in Hawaiʻi were notified by Washington that American bases were likely to be attacked somewhere in the Pacific. To everyone's surprise, the attack of December 7 was not confined to the Western Pacific but disastrously included Pearl Harbor.

What happened next resulted from the interplay of the M-Day Plan and the U.S. Army's insistence on martial law. Even though the army had supported the M-Day Plan, within a few hours of the attack it changed course and pressured the Territorial governor to declare undiluted army rule. Nonetheless, the army retained the network of civilian committees to participate in the martial law government, including the Food Committee on which Miwa served. The overall idea remained the same: total mobilization of resources and a desperate defense in case Japan attempted an invasion, which at the time seemed likely to occur at any moment.

Other than deploying army personnel to guard the perimeter of Oʻahu, nothing was more fundamental to this mobilization than feeding the population. Food production not only associated James with the right issue but also with the right people, chief among them the last of the great corporate titans of Hawai'i, Walter C. Dillingham. Dillingham chaired the Food Committee, not merely in name but in a personal and relentless pursuit of actually increasing the food supply.

Dillingham at the time sat atop a behemoth of a family business, Dillingham Corporation, which was often described as the sixth of the Big Five corporations. As number six, Dillingham Corporation was in many ways more aggressive and robust than the Big Five. It controlled much of the plantation land of leeward O'ahu, as well as the railroad that ran around the island. It also controlled much of the heavy machinery of construction and land development, as well as the wharfage of Honolulu Harbor. Through interlocking directorships, "Walter" also had a say in the affairs of the original Big Five corporations. He maintained his own lobbying office in Washington, D.C., and was a personal acquaintance of the president, Franklin D. Roosevelt, with whom he spoke by telephone about the Food Committee's work. Another member of the Food Committee was Y. Baron Goto, a blunt-spoken and scholarly Nisei who played a major role in agricultural education. Goto was one of perhaps two dozen members of the second generation who were in the inner circle of high trust with Army Intelligence and the FBI. All in all, the various community forces devoted to coping with the war formed tight webs. The army worked hand in glove with the FBI and the Honolulu Police Department, which worked hand in glove with Japanese Americans who were bent on fending off repression by proving their patriotism to the American nation. Miwa's membership in the Food Committee was a not insignificant footnote to the overall project.

The committee attempted to make a difference in the equation of available food and the demands of total war. One of the Pearl Harbor investigations says that on December 10, three days after the bombing, the committee held a meeting with the presidents of the Big Five, at which the plantation executives seemed less than eager to divert a significant portion of their lands or their workforces to raising vegetables. The agriculture of the Territory was about sugar, pineapple, and little else.

While the Food Committee attempted to set a direction, the martial law government struggled to find a balance between internal security and calming the Japanese community's fears of a mass internment. In these terms, Miwa was on a knife's edge. While he served the war effort in a prestigious way, he was carrying all sorts of baggage that was dangerous to his continued liberty. One was his imports from Japan. Closely related to this was his longtime leadership role in the Japanese Chamber of Commerce. There was additionally his unfortunate interview with *Nippu Jiji*, whose editor, Yasutaro Soga, and most of its staff had been swept up immediately by the FBI, not to mention the fact that his golfing friend, Kudo, had served as Japan's acting consul general in Honolulu. Finally, there was the question of the Miwa lifestyle in its totality: the incessant travel back and forth to Japan, the forays to the West Coast, and the matter of his settling Yoshio and the three children in Hiroshima. All in all, he was more a part of the Japanese immigrant community than the rapidly evolving and populous circles of Japanese Americans.

Despite being the third generation of Miwas with roots in Hawai'i, he was Japan born and therefore an alien, prevented by discriminatory anti-Asian immigration laws from becoming a naturalized U.S. citizen. Granted (for those who titrated the measurement of "Americanism"), James had attended Mid-Pacific Institute. He had been baptized a Christian and received a Christian name. He was widely acquainted and knew his way around many of the hidden corners of Honolulu. But, more to the point of the wartime arrests, he had not participated in the institutions of Americanization that had so deeply affected the attitudes and styles of the Japanese American generation—institutions such as the public schools, the University of Hawai'i, the YMCA, and, for some, the Reserve Officer Training program of the U.S. Army.

On December 7 and 8, the FBI arrested nearly four hundred people who were deemed to be "inimical" to the interests of the United States. That is, they had committed no crime—none was even hinted at—but they were regarded as too close for comfort to Imperial Japan and too influential in Hawai'i. The largest number were volunteer community representatives of the Japanese consulate, followed by Japanese schoolteachers, Buddhist priests, Shinto priests, the staffs of the Japanese-language press, and a small fraction of the American citizens of Japanese ancestry who had studied at length in Japan. The main figures of the Japanese Chamber of Commerce also were rolled up, with the exception of James Miwa.

Nonetheless, most people's first reaction was passably positive. Hawai'i had absorbed a terrible blow but coped. Calm prevailed. Japan did not attack again. Although many key figures in the Japan-connected elite had been rounded up, the threat of a mass internment was blunted. Contrary to signals from Washington, the army general governing Hawai'i, Delos C. Emmons, announced that as long as everyone behaved there would be no mass removal and incarceration.

This period of reassurance lasted for perhaps two or three weeks. At any rate, it was short-lived. Despite disclaimers by the FBI and Army Intelligence, unfounded rumors of sabotage and espionage spread. Word of the top-level arrests spread. Fear spread. With constitutional rights suspended, many wondered who might finger whom. As the weeks passed, the number of FBI arrests, backed by the army's administration of martial law, slowly rose—for reasons that were not made clear, either then or afterward.

Meanwhile, Dillingham and Baron Goto together performed as passionate advocates of Japanese farming interests. At one crucial point, Japanese farmers were stopped from their work by a military checkpoint at an ammunition dump on the leeward coast. Dillingham and Goto stormed up, demanding passage.

"Who are you?" a soldier asked.

"I am Walter Dillingham," he replied.

The way was cleared. Dillingham had a reputation from the 1920s of being anti-Japanese, and of contributing to political pressure for the Japanese Exclusion Act, but at some point he had become more sympathetic. In this sense he was a litmus test of an interwar shift, in which Japanese generally had become better acquainted and enjoyed increasingly effective relationships.

Dillingham became a touchpoint for Japanese Americans, who asked him to intercede with the federal government for their right to fight for America. In this meeting, it was said, tears welled up in Dillingham's eyes. Dillingham called the commander in chief of the Pacific, who called the martial law governor, who along with others under Dillingham's sway mounted the first major appeal for including Americans of Japanese ancestry—AJA, as they were being renamed—in armed combat on behalf of the United States.

All of this was to say that in the crisis, circles within circles influenced decisions, and Miwa was in the wrong circle at a bad moment. Although he was a third-generation resident, he was *not* an AJA—not even close—because of the family tradition of moving back and forth. His connections on the Territorial Food Committee were to no avail. On the contrary, his service to the committee may have made him unavoidably visible to the ardent American patriots who had taken over affairs in Hawai'i. A warrant for Miwa's arrest was issued on February 12. He was picked up the following day, which was the sixty-seventh day after the bombing of Pearl Harbor.

CHAPTER FOUR

Interned by the USA

Despite the absence of danger, internal security arrests were often made at gunpoint. Subjects were handcuffed in transit, typically with a driver and an armed guard in the front seat and a second armed officer in back. Per established procedure, James Seigo Miwa would have been booked and fingerprinted at the commandeered Yokohama Specie Bank, where six years previously he had bought a war bond issued by the Japanese Imperial government. Now the bank, ominously for Miwa's economic future, was under the control of the U.S. government's Alien Property Custodian.

From the bank building, Miwa would have been taken to the U.S. Immigration Station, a scene of misery that functioned as a way station into internment. From there, he was taken across a narrow channel in Honolulu Harbor to the army's Sand Island internment camp.

Reversing his twenty-five years of identity as James S. Miwa, the blizzard of U.S. Army forms now referred to him as Seigo Miwa. His fellow Issei also called him Seigo. After traveling the path of Americanization as a James, he was once again the Seigo of birth.[1]

All but a few of the internees were men, and most were of Japanese ancestry. They were separated from Honolulu by only a few hundred feet of water and yet, as one put it, "We felt as if we had drifted off to a faraway island."[2] Wrote another, "Without newspapers, we had no information about the outside world. So desperate were we that we were willing to steal them from the back pockets of the guards' pants."[3]

When Seigo Miwa arrived in the Sand Island camp, his fellow prisoners crowded around him, prompting him to recite every bit of war news he could recall.

One of the camp's most prolific writers, Kazuo Miyamoto, recorded one such scene as follows: "Now, let's have your report. What is the news from the Far East? Has Singapore capitulated?"[4] Fearing the camp commanders, the new arrival whispered his answers. A voice in the crowd told him to speak up: "Don't be afraid to talk aloud. This is Sand Island. You cannot sink any further."

The news for enthusiasts of Japan was uniformly good. By the date of Seigo's internment, Japan had invaded the Philippines, Guam, the Dutch East Indies, and Borneo. It held Taiwan, Korea, Manchuria, and about one-fourth of China, as well as numerous islands in the western and southern Pacific. Britain's colony at Singapore had just fallen to Japan, and the British Empire in Asia was crumbling. Japan had taken over the American base on Wake Island, which meant it credibly threatened to attack the Hawaiian Islands a second time and to follow through with a land invasion.

Like Seigo, most of the Issei at Sand Island were accustomed to leading others. They led businesses or institutions that served the broader community. They were a comparatively small, select group of individuals. Raised in a culture that constantly preached the importance of mutual obligation, they tended as a group to maintain a sense of obligation to Japan or to the Japanese immigrant community. Because the United States government had blocked their path to naturalized citizenship, they had no socially agreed-upon route, either legally or psychologically, by which to transfer their practice of loyalty to America. The rise of Japan as a first-rate world power was a matter of pride or, at the least, a balm to their wounded sensibilities. Japan had embraced them, sent teachers and priests to them, and maintained a vigorous consular operation to look out for them—this in contrast to the U.S. government, which had kept the door of citizenship shut, and which now had dragged them off from their homes and families, despite a complete absence of wrongdoing, and locked them up.

Seigo's life was exceptionally divided, unusually nuanced. He was not a first-generation immigrant but a third. The facts of his Christian baptism and his missionary-school education meant that he was to some considerable degree an outsider by the standards of Japan. At age eighteen, he had registered with his draft board for potential service in the American army, then renewed his registration three years later. In the aftermath of Japan's attack on Pearl Harbor, he had served Hawai'i at the moment of crisis through the Territorial Food Committee. He had multiple businesses in Hawai'i and a branch office in San Francisco. His three generations of residence and the long arc of Miwa business history made for a greater than average investment in Hawai'i.

Nonetheless he was a citizen of Japan alone. He was the son of a Japanese war veteran and the grandson of a *samurai*. He owned an export business, a rubber factory, and an entire neighborhood in Hiroshima. His wife and children had lived in Hiroshima for the past decade. He had come back to Hawai'i on one of the last two ships, but he had not brought his family with him, when many of the other passengers had done so.

His last opportunity to defend himself was a hearing of a sort conducted on March 18, 1942. It was held at Fort Shafter, the headquarters of the United States Army in the Pacific. Shafter was a fort built at the turn of the century that spoke through each board and nail of the Territory of Hawai'i's colonial origins. The white frame buildings were laid out on a large U-shaped drive that was lined by palms. These were not the swaying coconut-bearing palms of unpredictable shape and grace but the rigidly vertical no-nut royal palm.

The hearing consisted of three civilians and an army officer who served as administrator and recorder. All took an oath to perform their

Although described as an internee, James Seigo Miwa and his companions were booked and their mugshots taken as if they were common criminals, February 1942. (U.S. National Archives)

duties with the help of God. The civilians were accomplished citizens who would have been acquainted with people of Japanese ancestry. Edward N. Sylva was an attorney and later an Attorney General of the Territorial government. David Y. K. Akana was a Territorial senator. Mark A. Robinson was a major landowner. They served to dignify an extralegal situation pursuant to general orders of the martial law government. It was an illusion of due process when, in reality, the real processes of constitutional government, such as *habeas corpus* and the right to a jury trial of one's peers, had been suspended. Nonetheless, the idea of hearing boards was sufficiently superior to the wholesale, racially based eradication of people from the West Coast as to occasionally draw positive remarks from future scholars.

On closer examination, the statement of the military's base of authority reflected the makeshift nature of the martial law project in Hawai'i. Paragraph One cited the authority of Special Order 320, Paragraph 33, issued on December 19, as amended by Paragraph 6 of Special Order 326, issued on December 25, as further amended by Paragraph 26 of Special Order 332, issued on December 31. The stated purpose was to hear evidence and make recommendations "as to the internment of enemy aliens, dual citizens and citizens."

An FBI agent, John Harold Hughes, was sworn as a witness to present what he knew about Seigo Miwa. Meanwhile Miwa was kept outside the room, preventing him from listening to what was being said about him that might, in the minds of the hearing officers, have warranted his being locked up indefinitely.

Hughes recounted Senkichi Miwa's migration to Hawai'i and the development of the Miwa stores, along with the fact that Senkichi was deceased and his widow Kiyo lived in Japan, as did Seigo Miwa's wife and three children. Further, Hughes described four of the numerous trips Seigo had made to Japan, including the long stays between 1935 and 1938, which were tied to the death of Senkichi, and Seigo's last trip to Japan in the spring of 1941.

Hughes identified two of the three stores in Honolulu and another in San Francisco. He said a fourth, located in Hiroshima, was no longer operating because of the war. A search of Miwa's residence and stores in Honolulu "failed to develop anything of significance other than the location of five $1000 imperial Japanese Government bonds," which Miwa had bought in 1935.

Hughes took note of Miwa's service to the Territory's Food Committee, but then gave it a negative twist. "He was reported as a person who should not be placed in that position because of his connections with Japan," Agent Hughes said.

That was all. "We have no further information regarding him." Following the FBI agent's seven-minute presentation, Hughes was excused.

Hughes's statement was the only clue as to how Seigo had come to the attention of the authorities and why he had been arrested. If his service on the Food Committee was essentially all the security agencies knew about him, then it was his public service that had brought him down. Conceivably, one of Seigo's acquaintances had led someone to look at his life history, and that person had concluded that James Seigo Miwa was, in the vocabulary of the day, "too Japanese." His name had then gone to the FBI.

When Miwa was ushered into the hearing room, the proceeding immediately stumbled over the question of his name.

When asked by the recorder to state his name, he replied, "Seigo Miwa."

"Are you also known as James Seigo Miwa?" the recorder asked.

"I usually sign it J. S. Miwa," he replied.

Recorder: "Will you spell your name?"

The internee, as he was referred to in the record, asked, "I beg your pardon?"

Recorder: "Will you spell your name?"

Internee: "J-A-M-E-S S-E-I-G-O M-I-W-A."

The recorder then asked if he had been served with a warrant of arrest.

No, he replied.

Nonetheless, the recorder directed the record to show that Miwa had been served with a warrant.

Recorder: "This is a military hearing."

Internee: "Yes."

Recorder: "And is accorded you as a matter of justice."

Miwa was given the option of testifying under oath, or without taking an oath, or responding in writing.

Internee: "I want to answer now. Under oath."

Did he want to call character witnesses?

No, he said, making a serious mistake, given the number of prestigious haole whom Miwa might have called as witnesses on his behalf.

The basic facts of family and business were reconstructed. The recorder belabored the fact that Miwa's children were dual citizens. "The fact that you registered them with the Japanese Consul indicates that you wanted them to be Japanese rather than Americans," the recorder said, presuming something that was not necessarily true.

"That depends on the children when they grow up and decide what to do," Miwa replied. Clearly, he was saying that the purpose of dual citizenship was to preserve a child's options in adulthood.

Board members then asked questions.

Did he have any friends or relatives serving in Japan's armed forces? No.

In his trips to Japan, had he visited battlefields in China? No.

Were his trips for family or business? Both.

Did he have a branch store in Japan? "We had it, yes."

Was he Buddhist, Shinto, or Christian? Christian.

The questioner was skeptical. "Christian?"

"Yes." Miwa said he was a baptized Christian.

Had he ever purchased Japanese war bonds? Miwa said he had done so, eight or nine years earlier, through a local bank. He described buying four bonds from Yokohama Specie Bank and one bond from a second Japanese bank. The bonds then had been deposited in Bishop National Bank. His description of eight or nine years was a slight stretch. The reality was closer to six years.

What did he think of the "new doctrine of the new order in Greater East Asia?"

"I don't know," Miwa replied. "I can't say anything. I am not a politician."

"You have never taken much stock in it?" a board member (unidentified in the record) asked. "You have never studied it or given it much thought?"

"No," Miwa replied, "I have not."

What did he think of Japan's invasion of Manchuria?

"Well," Miwa replied, "I have no idea at all."

This went on, leading to the question of questions: Which side did he want to win the war?

"I can't say," Miwa replied. "It is pretty hard to say. I have been raised here, you see, most of the time my life has been here." In this, he defaulted to the idea of Hawai'i being home base, of it being the independent country of Marujiro's and Senkichi's arrivals and the semi-separate territory of his own experience.

"You find it very hard to say?"

"I can't say."

"You can't say?"

"No."

The board member asked again, "You cannot tell us whether you would like to see America or Japan win?"

In future tense, Miwa replied, "I can't tell you which side will win unless I am God."

Board member: "I am not asking you that. Which side would you like to see win this war?"

Miwa: "I can't say."

Board member: "Why is that?"

Miwa: "It puts me in a hard position. I have been here a long time and I know so many people here and I don't have many friends in Japan. Lots of friends here but still I am a subject of Japan. I can't say only unless you force me then I got to say, unless I commit *harakiri*"— that is, unless he disemboweled himself with a sword.

Despite the continued prompting to predict a winner in the war, he stuck to the idea of neutrality.

"You would rather not answer the question?"

"Yes."

Would he bear arms against Japan in defense of Hawai'i?

"No," Miwa said, "I don't think so."

Was there anything more he would like to say? "No, I don't think so."

One more question: had he ever bought U.S. war bonds? Answer: no. Question: why not? Answer: before the war he had credit on which to operate his San Francisco store but now he had none. All his money was going to keeping the store going.

A board member then recited the surprise nature of the attack on Pearl Harbor. Did Miwa not think it was dishonorable?

"Well, I don't know about international law," Miwa said. "I can't say." Well, the board member retorted, it was common sense that you don't attack someone from behind. Did he agree with that or did he have no views on the matter?

"I have no views on the matter," Miwa said.

Where had he made most of his money?

Mostly in Hawai'i, Miwa said. What he had made in Japan "is from my grandfathers."

"The internee is excused," the recorder said.

The board issued three findings: First, Miwa was a citizen of Japan. Second, he was "loyal to Japan and dis-loyal [*sic*] to the United States." Third, "he is not engaged in any subversive activities." On the basis of these findings, the board recommended that he be interned for the duration of the war.

All four members signed the finding, which then was forwarded to the head of the three U.S. intelligence agencies—the FBI, Army Intelligence, and Navy Intelligence. All of these had a hand in the internment question. The next transaction was apparently *pro forma* but dated March 23, five days after the hearing officers had directed Miwa's incarceration. Lt. Col. George Bicknell, assistant head of Army Intelligence in Hawai'i; Captain I. H. Mayfield, head of the Navy's District Intelligence Office; and Robert L. Shivers, FBI Special Agent in Charge of the Honolulu field office, signed in concurrence with the recommendation.

Of the three, it was Shivers who had been empowered by the martial law government to have the last say on whether someone was interned. The next day, March 24, Col. Thomas H. Green, executive officer of the martial law government, signed the order of internment. From mid-1940 forward, Green had served as the chief attorney of the Hawaiian army command. During that time, he had written the general orders of martial law under which Seigo Miwa had been arrested and put before a hearing board. Green had organized the board and now finally sent Miwa into internment. Effectively he had exercised in his single person the legislative, executive, and judicial responsibilities of a civilian government.

When it was said that constitutional rights were suspended under martial law, James Seigo Miwa was an example of what that meant. The "hearing" was, by the narrowest of definitions, quasi-judicial, but it was flawed from the outset. Miwa was not allowed access to the accusations. If he had been represented by an attorney, as was his right, the tone of the event would have been different. The rhetorical presumptions of the questions were objectionable—indeed many of them were outrageous by the rules of logic. The shading of the questions all had to do with his attachments to Japan. There was no acknowledgment of the fact that he had been a good citizen of Hawai'i for many years. There was no acknowledgment of his American education or the fact that as a young man he had registered for the U.S. draft. There was no effective presentation of him being caught in the middle, an alien of long standing and long relationship, who had been denied naturalization by American law.

Further, in moments where Miwa seemed not to grasp the nuance of adjectives or verb tense, a half-decent attorney could have jumped in and pressed for clarity. When Miwa was asked which side he wanted to win the war, an attorney could have pointed out to the board that Miwa had answered by saying only God knew who would actually win the war, a *non sequitur.*

Most elementally, a vigorous defense would have pointed to the complete absence of wrongdoing. A vigorous defense would have challenged the implication that in some way Miwa was a threat to the community and to the war effort. Assuming all the suggestions and innuendos about him had substance, did any of them warrant his being locked up and taken away? Did any of them warrant his being interned in wartime?

On the record, all the FBI knew was that Miwa was in the import business, that he did business in Japan, that his wife and children were living in Japan, and that despite repeated prompting he had declined to budge from a neutral statement regarding the war. If the FBI was aware of the most problematic points of Miwa's past—the January 1940 *Nippu Jiji* interview, the rubber manufacturing company in Hiroshima, and his close relationship to the Japanese consul—these were not presented.

In light of what was at stake, Miwa's honesty was astonishing. If he was going to talk his way out of internment, he would have begun and ended his pleading on a statement of heartfelt fervor for America and the American war effort. He would have flatly answered that he wanted America to win. He would have denounced Japan's conduct of war as treacherous and cowardly. He would have underscored the fact that he was the third generation of Miwas to live in Hawai'i, and that his children were U.S. citizens. He would have conversationally dealt out additional biographical details of the sort that ethnocentric white Americans found so reassuring, such as his education at Mills (Mid-Pacific) Institute, his baptism, his service to the Food Committee, and his trusting relationships with haole of the island establishment.

He had a good story to tell. Under the circumstances, it was a story to sell, but he was too polite to dredge it up. In Japanese culture, brevity of words and a certain reserve were to be admired. He was not a salesman.

LIFE AT THE SAND ISLAND CAMP was degrading. Prisoners were herded into formation and forced to strip off their clothes. They then were searched while standing naked in the cold rains of Hawai'i's winter. Throughout Miwa's stay at Sand Island, the prisoners continued to live in stinking canvas army tents. The landscape was barren. As the winter

gave way to spring, the sun beat down. The mess hall often served ancient remnants of pork laced with beans.

Soon after Miwa's arrival, an air-raid siren shrieked. People began
running, and Miwa was shoved down into a slit trench, which the prisoners had been required to dig. Rumors spread through the camp that
if Japan launched an invasion, the U.S. Army planned to release poison
gas.[5] Everyone carried gas masks at all times. While this was required
of the entire population under martial law, the army released tear gas
on the Sand Island prisoners in air-raid drills. If the prisoners got into
their masks quickly enough, no harm was done. If they fumbled, the gas
made their faces and eyes sore for hours.

One of Miwa's fellow internees was to write that individuals who
were interned on December 7 tended to accept their fate as sealed by
the prewar FBI investigations. In contrast, those arrested later, such as
Miwa, wondered if they were victims of a whispered allegation of dis-
loyalty. The imagined whisperers were called dogs, or *inu* in Japanese.
The word became widely current in the entire Japanese community.
Who was *inu?*

While Miwa suffered his Sand Island imprisonment in silence,
several of his companions later wrote about their experiences. A journalist from Hawai'i Island, Otokichi Ozaki, said that of the five camps
he was locked in during the war, Sand Island was the worst.

Subjects of Japan had been told all their lives that Japan had
never lost a war and was therefore unbeatable. At Pearl Harbor and in
the early months of the war, nothing happened to challenge this article
of faith. The idea of victorious war took on a reality of its own. After
America won the colossal sea battle at Midway Island in June of 1942,
a story spread in camp that actually Japan had won.[6] In effect, the
army's news blackout inflicted a terrible cost, because it further separated the internees from the real world. In the absence of factual news,
they believed what they wanted to believe.

Miwa spent over three months at Sand Island. During that time,
the camp population went up and down. At first there were five hundred or so people. Almost immediately a third of them were called out
of formation and shipped to the U.S. mainland. The first shipment was
on February 21, only nine days after Miwa's arrest. The proximity of
his arrest to the shipment raises the question of whether his and other
new arrests were, effectively, replacement arrests. Without doubt, this
was the case with Neighbor Island prisoners, who were shipped to Sand
Island immediately after the first group of Oʻahu internees was shipped

out. Like a hotel, the Sand Island camp took in new occupants as previous occupants departed.

When Miwa was booked into Sand Island, turmoil was at a high pitch. Just as the United States was trying to monitor Japan's prisoner camps, Japan was attempting to get neutral-nation observers into the Sand Island camp to monitor for Geneva Convention violations. Contention over living conditions, diet, visitation, and general rough treatment was ongoing and unresolved. The involuntary residents of Sand Island first had been referred to as arrestees and then as prisoners. In an attempt to soften the blow, the martial law governor announced they were not prisoners but detainees. Miwa nonetheless would thereafter be treated as a prisoner. Throughout his stay on Sand Island, he lived under armed guard, confined by a sharply delineated barbed wire perimeter. His daily routine and movements were militarized. On command, he fell into formation and marched in formation.

After the first shipment, another one hundred sixty-six prisoners were moved to the West Coast a month later. Two more months passed. Then the camp members were ordered to stand in formation, with a new reading of the lists. Seigo Miwa's name was among them.

On May 23, five and one-half months into the war, Miwa was one of a hundred and nine prisoners who were transported ashore and marched along the waterfront in Honolulu under a heavy armed guard to the S.S. *Maui*. They were locked in the hold, under guard. The following day the ship sailed eastward.

Prisoners were split into groups of eight or ten and assigned to small compartments. They were not allowed on deck for exercise or air. Latrines stank and were available only at three-hour intervals. Many of the men were old and suffered from deteriorating control of their bladders. They banged on the iron door, pleading to relieve themselves, only to be ignored. In desperation, they sometimes urinated into a can or defecated in a small sink.

During this period Japan's submarines freely navigated the ocean between Hawai'i and the West Coast. This forced the *Maui* to employ a zigzag course that stretched its time at sea to nine days. The ship sailed into San Francisco Bay on June 1, 1942, in the sixth month of the war. Immediately, the prisoners were transferred to the offshore immigration station, Angel Island, which many Asians previously had thought of as the western gate of American opportunity.

At Angel Island, the U.S. government's personnel record identified Miwa as an "Alien Enemy or Prisoner of War." He was fingerprinted

SOUTHERN PACIFIC DEPOT, LORDSBURG, N. M.

The Lordsburg train station was the point of James Seigo Miwa's arrival into long-term internment.

and photographed face-on and in profile, as if he were a criminal. The Angel Island paperwork said he had arrived at "Headquarters Prisoner of War Enclosure." After "Name of Prisoner," Miwa was given an "Internment Serial No.," ISN-HJ-291-CI. With a bit of dark humor, the journalist Yasutaro Soga, similarly interned, wrote that if a person in confinement is assigned a number, it does not bode well for his future. Miwa now wore a uniform with his serial number on it, along with big letters that said "POW." After a week at Angel Island, he was ferried with his group back across the San Francisco Bay, loaded onto a train with its blinds pulled, and moved to Fort Sam Houston in San Antonio, Texas. Ten days later, he was shipped into the desert of southern New Mexico at a desolate whistle stop named Lordsburg.

His train arrived in midafternoon. The temperature was one hundred and ten degrees. He was lined up in a military formation, one of four abreast, and marched through the desert to the internment camp. He passed under watchtowers and through barbed wire fences, which were guarded by armed soldiers.[7]

The camp was built for three thousand men, who were divided into three battalions of one thousand men each. Battalions in turn were divided into companies of two hundred and fifty. Miwa could see, strangely, that his barracks was tethered to the ground by thick wires.

Their purpose was to keep the makeshift building from blowing away in a windstorm. The inside of the barracks was covered with dirt and sand. Miwa and his companions swept out their new quarters. A whirlwind came along and again coated everything with dirt. The men wet their handkerchiefs and tied them around their nostrils, like bandits, but the dirt was suffocating.

Storms sometimes blew up several times a day, cutting visibility to a few feet, and even to inches. Around the windy side of the building, dirt and sand piled like snowdrifts, accreting into perilous pinnacles, then toppling, only to rise again. One prisoner wrote, "Everyone conceded defeat to the sandstorms."[8]

When Miwa lay down to sleep, he heard coyotes howling outside the barracks. Inmates gnashed their teeth and talked in their sleep. Sometimes they wept. Personality traits became magnified. Some people became jumpy. Some became boastful and grandiose. Others withdrew. The courtly Soga was disgusted by the deteriorating quality of conversation. "To relieve the boredom," he wrote, "more and more men engaged in filthy talk."

Table manners suffered. Among a people known for their adherence to courtesies, certain individuals would reach across the table, grabbing food and salt. For amusement, some of the men captured horned toads and made them into pets.

"Eat. Sleep. Wake up. Eat. Sleep. Wake up," Ozaki wrote. "A life cut off from everything in the world. The unbearable monotony of a life without variation seems to slowly warp our minds."

When the first winter came, the wind intensified and the sandstorms worsened. The temperature fluctuated between a baking heat in the day and freezing cold at night.

On average, the men in camp had functioned in their previous lives as exceptionally vigorous individuals. They were accustomed to asserting themselves and being acknowledged for their status and their accomplishments. "I feel we are becoming addlebrained," Ozaki wrote, "our thinking ability diminished."[9]

"We will become living corpses," he predicted. "Everyone's eyes are beginning to look like those of dead fish."

In the stereotyping of this FBI wave of internees, the older and more culturally Japanese men would be sentimentally remembered for their stamina, their poetry, their lectures, classes, and folk art. A narrative was to develop about interned individuals battling stoically, serving one another as companions and friends. While elements of this narrative were true, as far as they went, the symptoms of deterioration and despair were sanitized. No one wanted to talk about life in camp—not the men, not their families, and not the U.S. government.

From what can be discerned, Seigo Miwa maintained his balance. He was chosen by his barracks and then by his block of barracks to serve as their leader. This meant taking care of and representing his jurisdiction, communicating with his constituents, and commanding the group in the formations required of them. It also meant interacting with other block leaders.

He was a member of the third group from Hawai'i to arrive at Lordsburg. When Soga's group, the fifth group, arrived, Miwa and his comrades rallied at the gate. They pooled their resources and gave each of the new arrivals a soda.

George Hoshida of Hilo, a sketch artist, was part of Miwa's group. He drew a pen and ink picture of Miwa at Lordsburg in early August 1942. Where Miwa had been described in his 1940 *Nippu Jiji* interview as being in his late thirties but looking younger, he now looked all of his forty-five years. He wore the round spectacles that were popular with Japanese of the time. His closely cropped hair rose to a peak above his brow. Hoshida drew deep lines on Miwa's forehead, on both sides of his mouth, and across his chin. Miwa no longer looked so bland and tailored. He was more rugged and engaging, as if confinement had given him character.

In the context of the camp, he was among the younger and more vigorous. He was bilingual. He had deep roots in Hawai'i and deep roots in Japan. He was a business success on the American model. When delusion was rampant, he maintained a realistic understanding of the tides of the war. Although completely cut off from family, he realized they were in mortal danger.

LIFE IN LORDSBURG PROCEEDED IN AN atmosphere of tension and occasional violence. When a new shipment of prisoners arrived, two elderly members of the shipment were left under guard at the Lordsburg train station, too ill to march across the desert. A U.S. soldier shot them both. One died on the spot. The second died the next morning at dawn. When the case was belatedly investigated, the guard claimed the two men were trying to escape. He was exonerated.[10] An officer who explained the verdict to the prisoners of Lordsburg said, "If I had to give an opinion, I'd say the two men committed suicide."

In a situation where any indication of loyalty to one's citizenship

Fellow internee George Hoshida, widely known for his camp art, sketched James Seigo Miwa shortly after his arrival in Lordsburg internment camp, August, 1942. (Japanese American National Museum [Gift of June Hoshida Honma, Sandra Hoshida, and Carole Hoshida Kanada])

in Japan potentially brought down disastrous discrimination on the entire Japanese-ancestry population in America, most of whom were American citizens, later writers would mince words about the national passions of an element of Issei internees in the FBI camps. Those who wrote in the moment were more forthcoming. Soga, for one, bluntly described Japanese nationalist sentiment at Lordsburg as rampant.

Soga's group put together a list of Hawai'i Japanese in the camp. They wrote a militant preface about which Soga later expressed embarrassment. "December 7, 1941!" their statement began. "Black smoke rose and explosive sounds reverberated over Pearl Harbor in the early morning. They not only woke the people of Hawai'i but also announced the arrival of a new age. It was the first day of the great leap into a new world. It was the day when a bright light began to shine on the futures of one billion Asians."

Echoing Japan's propaganda, the statement described Japan as Asia's liberator. The setting sun of the desert over Lordsburg caused the men to "tearfully give thanks that we were born in Japan."[11] The statement was dated January 1943 and was signed by all members of the fifth, sixth, and seventh groups from Hawai'i.

Against the searing heat, the pro-Japan element demanded an increasingly unthinking loyalty, in which factual analysis was suspended. As future events were to prove, Miwa was unwilling to do this.

CHAPTER FIVE

Traded to Japan

Eventually Seigo Miwa would be dismissive, almost cavalier, about his internment experience. He would say that he never went hungry. He was never mistreated. He was even paid a little for the work he performed.

He was tough, and he realized that many other people had a worse time in war than he. But it also seems likely that he gave short shrift to his story for the future benefit of his children, and because of the fact that they were both Japanese and American. He conducted himself in a way that, he hoped, would keep their options open, psychologically and emotionally.

Beginning in the spring of 1942, the question before him was whether he and others might be released from the camp and returned to Japan. The repatriation debate within camp was inflamed by word that the United States and Japan were negotiating a possible exchange of civilian prisoners. In that context, Miwa and his comrades danced at the end of long strings.

Although Miwa left behind only a meager record of his life in Lordsburg, others partially filled it. Soga, Ozaki, Hoshida, and Sui-kei Furuya all wrote at length about the tone and events of life in the camp.[1] As an occasional character in their accounts, Miwa recurs, but as a silent presence. In Furuya's departure from Sand Island, Miwa is watching from the second-floor window of the immigration building. He leads his barracks, then multiple barracks. He is sketched. In the Japanese Chamber of Commerce list of members who were interned, he appears as "Shogo" Miwa.

Given the course of future events, some aspects of his life seem certain. For example, it seems certain that he would have participated in the debate over repatriation to Japan. It was a singular camp subject. "When I arrived at Lordsburg," Soga wrote, "those who were already there from Hawai'i were eager to return to Japan. They recommended that I do the same."

Soga was a contemporary of Seigo's father, Senkichi. Soga, who had initially worked in a plantation store, filled out the paperwork of his fellow immigrants and helped them write letters home, predating the consular volunteers who were of such interest to the FBI. He had risen in the Japanese newspaper world of Honolulu by writing about the 1905 war between Japan and Russia. He then transformed *Nippu Jiji* into one of the leading Japanese newspapers in the Territory of Hawai'i.[2] In 1919, he had championed a pioneering Territory-wide strike of plantation workers, for which he was jailed by unconstitutional means. Soga was arrested again at gunpoint on December 7 and thrust into a blackened room. He could scarcely find a place to stand, let alone sit or lie. With the light of December 8, he realized that most of the prisoners were, like himself, prominent Issei. Most were acquainted with one another.[3] Unlike Miwa, Soga had requested an attorney at his hearing, but the attorney's presence was not enough to keep him out of long-term internment. Following a grim stint at Sand Island, he was shipped to Lordsburg. Choking on the dust, freezing in the cold, at age sixty-nine he carefully made notes on his journey, which later he would publish as a uniquely revealing book.[4]

Soga portrayed a camp under the overall sway of Japanese nationalism but torn between fanaticism and rationality. The powerful culture of Japan weighed heavily. To pass the time, Soga played *go,* the Japanese board game of strategy. He wrote hundreds of haiku and *tanka* poems, some of excellent quality. A group of internees formed a theater troupe and enacted *Chūshingura,* the story of the forty-seven Ronin warriors who gave up their lives to avenge their master's death.[5] During a lecture, which Soga attended, a Shintō priest proposed that after Japan won the war, all Japanese in the United States should move to the South Pacific. The priest also argued against the U.S. Army's conscription of Nisei, a second major subject of disputation in the camp.

Because Soga was a Japanese citizen, he reasoned he was duty bound to be pro-Japan, but on the question of Nisei participation in the U.S. military, he parted ways with the hardline nationalists. The U.S. Army's soon-to-be-famous 100th Infantry Battalion had been formed from prewar Japanese American draftees in Hawai'i. The Hawai'i contingent at Lordsburg often had sons in the U.S. military, and almost everyone from Hawai'i knew of someone of Japanese ancestry in American uniform. Soga argued that the question of Nisei service in the U.S.

Armed Forces should be left to the Nisei. He said Japanese in Hawai'i were in an entirely different situation from Japanese on the U.S. mainland. He held to the idea that citizenship determined loyalties. "As long as they are American citizens," he argued, "the *nisei* are obliged to serve their country."

For advancing this view, Soga was branded as pro-American. He complained bitterly that "sentiments that seem the least bit anti-American would find favor among the internees."[6]

Certain internees were designated to sift through whatever information was available and to announce it as news. "Whenever there was good news from the Imperial headquarters," Soga wrote, "everyone went wild, although what we were hearing at the time was mostly propaganda."[7]

Soga had invested his entire adult life in Hawai'i, and despite his pro-Japan sentiments he was in no mood to return to the country of his birth. Despite the enthusiasm for repatriation he reported around him, he wrote that he did not personally give it a second thought.

A SECOND ACQUAINTANCE OF MIWA, THE writer Ozaki, told a more deeply conflicted story. Ozaki had been brought to Hawai'i by his immigrant parents when he was twelve. He had gone to work at an early age on a Japanese language newspaper, the *Hilo Mainichi*. He then taught at an independent Japanese language school. It was community-based, as distinct from the schools administered from Japan by Buddhist sects. He brought the Japanese language to life for his students by discussing Washington and Lincoln. To excite their interest in literature, he gave them classical European and American novels.

He also served the Japanese consulate as a volunteer community representative. Like Soga before him, Ozaki provided translation and writing services to semi-literate Japanese immigrants who lived beyond the day-to-day working radius of the Japanese consulate in Honolulu.

In the fear-ridden semantics of the FBI, Ozaki was a consular agent. The FBI agent who investigated him prior to the war accurately described Ozaki's consular work as essentially humanitarian. The agent also was impressed by the fact that, on the advice of a language school official, Ozaki had resigned from his teaching job in the spring of 1941. Nonetheless he was arrested and told to pack for three or four days.

He was locked in an army camp near the Hawai'i Island volcano. When space opened at Sand Island, he was moved to O'ahu. "Is this what America is about?" an inflamed Ozaki asked. "It made me reconsider the greatness of America, where I had been raised over the decades."[8]

He ate greasy food from a greasy mess kit, which was washed by dipping it in water and quickly passing it on to a fellow inmate. Two prisoners shared one water cup. One man drank from one side of the cup and one drank from the other side. Armed soldiers were stationed every few feet, occasionally growling, "Goddam Japs."

Accustomed to eating with chopsticks, Ozaki was given a knife, fork, and spoon, which as metal objects became the subject of strip searches.

The inmates referred to the world outside the camp as *shaba,* which means *the corrupt world.* After one hundred days in camp, Ozaki looked into the mirror at his unshaven face and asked, "Are you me?"

"I owed a debt of gratitude [to the United States]," Ozaki was to write, "but now I felt I was free of my obligation." He interpreted the actions of the U.S. government as saying, "Even though you have lived in Hawai'i for many years and have devoted yourself to the United States, we do not believe you. You are Japanese."[9]

As with Miwa at Lordsburg, Ozaki was familiar with the shooting death of a fellow prisoner. While passing through Fort Sill, Oklahoma, a compatriot from the Big Island named Kanesaburo Oshima lost control of himself, climbed the inner fence, and then tried to climb a second fence. His fellow prisoners ran alongside the armed guards, shouting that Oshima had lost his senses. They begged the guards not to shoot. One guard fired several shots but missed. A second guard shot Oshima in the back of the head. He owned a service station in the South Kona district of Hawai'i Island, as well as a car dealership, a barber shop, and an ice shop. He was the father of eleven children. In camp, he had cut the other men's hair without charge.[10] He was fifty-eight years old.

Gripped by despair, Ozaki decided to repatriate to Japan. A tortured correspondence with his wife followed. Mrs. Ozaki, an American citizen, dutifully wrote that the family must stay together at all costs, and therefore she and their four American children would go with him to Japan. With her husband in internment, she and the children, along with Ozaki's parents, had moved from Hawai'i Island to Honolulu, where they lived with her brother-in-law, who had six children of his own.

Through her letters, it became clear that Mrs. Ozaki, contrary to her professed stance, actually did not want to go to Japan. While repeating her willingness to go with her husband, she obliquely stated that she had consulted friends who urged her to remain in Hawai'i.[11] "I have discussed the matter with Father and Mother," she wrote to her husband, "but they do not wish to return to Japan." She supposed they had become accustomed to life in Hawai'i. To this she added, "We purchased land here with the intention of staying forever, so I have regrets about leaving it behind."[12] Thereafter, Ozaki abandoned repatriation in favor of meeting his wife and children in a reunification camp in Jerome, Arkansas, which turned out to be yet another horrendously difficult experience.

CONTRARY TO THE CHEERFUL ACCOUNT THAT Miwa was to give his children, he was surrounded by such deeply depressing circumstances. The George Hoshida who drew the ink sketch of Miwa had not been immediately fearful of arrest after the Pearl Harbor attack. However, he belonged to a martial arts association that practiced judo, kendo, and archery, and he taught judo. Worse yet, the group's constitution contained a ritual statement of loyalty to the emperor. The weeks after December 7 came and went, and nothing happened. Just as he began to relax, he was arrested. He believed he had been fingered by an FBI informer.

Hoshida left behind a pregnant wife and three children. The oldest child was an eight-year-old girl who, as an infant, had been in a car wreck and could not see or walk and suffered from impaired hearing. Some time after Hoshida was shipped to Lordsburg, a social worker advised his wife that the little girl be placed in a home for the disabled, Waimano Home in Pearl City. There she drowned in a bathtub.[13]

In camp, Hoshida raised his voice for the internees who were older and less fit than he. He took it upon himself to speak against forced work in the sun in hundred-degree heat. When Hoshida spoke to a guard, the guard pointed his gun at him and ordered him to step back. Hoshida persisted. "These people are ministers and Japanese school teachers and prominent Japanese leaders in the Japanese community," he said. "So, they [are] not used to this kind of work." He asked the guard to go easy. The guard said he didn't know anything about the internees but he did know that his own twin brother had been killed at Pearl Harbor. Hoshida said he was sorry to hear this. "And I start talking," Hoshida recounted, "and then he soften[ed] up." The guard moved the old Japanese men into the shade.

The internees argued that if they were to be treated as prisoners of war under the Geneva Convention, they could not be forced to do slave labor, which they interpreted as working outside their barracks area.

They went on strike and were placed under lock and key for a month. A representative of the embassy of Spain, as a neutral nation, conducted a fact-finding mission. He came to no immediate conclusion but urged the men to go back to work until he could arrive at one. In the interim, the camp commander was replaced, and work conditions improved.

Although depressed, Hoshida decided against repatriation, opting instead for eventual family reunification at the Jerome camp.

It appears that of the three hundred and fifty men from Hawai'i in Lordsburg, about one hundred and fifty asked to be repatriated to Japan.

THE NEXT QUESTION THIS GROUP FACED, Miwa among them, was how they might return to Japan in the midst of deadly combat. Oddly, the governments of Japan and the United States had discussed prisoner exchanges well before the onset of fighting. To facilitate such a discussion, the U.S. State Department had created a low-profile bureau called the Special War Problems Division. This was twenty-six months in advance of the actual war.[14] The Special Division was a subset of the State Department.

In October 1940, the State Department advised the families of American government personnel in the Far East to return to the United States. America's ambassador to Japan, Joseph Grew, wanted to spread the word quietly, so as not to alarm Japan. He then reported that Japan nonetheless was alarmed. By the State Department's count, there were 295 people of American interest in Japan and many more in China— 6,700 by the U.S. government count, plus 1,280 in British Hong Kong. There were 476 in what then was the Dutch East Indies, and a few others scattered around elsewhere, not to mention uncounted thousands in the Philippines, which then was an American colony.[15] In sum, America had many thousands of overseas civilians in the path of the Asian land war. Crucially to the future of prisoner exchange, Japan had only its diplomatic personnel in the United States and a relatively small number of others who were of much interest to the Japanese government, most of whom were businessmen.

ON JULY 26, 1941, PRESIDENT ROOSEVELT froze Japanese credits in American banks (which must have alarmed Miwa, who was then in Japan with his family). In the months that followed, the two governments negotiated the arrival and departure of ocean liners evacuating people to their respective homelands. Prominently these were the *Coolidge* on the American side and, on the Japanese side, the *Tatsuta Maru,* the ship on which Miwa had returned to Hawai'i.

The voyages of the *Coolidge* and the *Tatsuta Maru* were sources of prewar friction. At one point, the FBI suspected a Japanese national of taking several million dollars in securities out of the United States, in violation of the President's freeze on assets. American agents boarded the *Tatsuta Maru,* causing the Japanese government to charge that the United States had seized the ship. Japan, for its part, interfered with the movements of the *Coolidge* by restricting when and where it could pick up American nationals for transport to the United States.

Although the problems of prisoner exchange during active warfare would become much greater, the prewar bickering foreshadowed the difficulties to come. In October 1941, the Japanese Embassy opened discussions with Washington on repatriation of its citizens in the event of war. As late as November 21, 1941, Japan's ambassador informed the American secretary of state that the *Tatsuta Maru* was to sail on December 2 to pick up more passengers in Japan for shipment to the United States. By this time, many of Japan's corporate businesses on the U.S. West Coast were closing, and their employees were returning to Japan.

As a result of such advance preparations, the United States presented a proposal to Japan for a prisoner exchange the day after the Pearl Harbor attack. The proposal was routed through a friendly noncombatant nation, Switzerland, which gave the proposal to Spain, a noncombatant on friendly terms with Japan.

Japan worried about being cheated. On December 16, the Japanese government came back with a list of people they wanted in a trade. Foremost were government officials. Against an imagined exchange of equals, Japan profiled additional prospects for a swap in terms of "family background, social status, and education." In context of bloody war, their attempted weighing of prisoner against prisoner was true to form—a throwback to Japan's longstanding goal of being treated as an equal with the Western powers.[16]

Although Japan did in fact want its diplomats returned, much heavier pressure fell on the American side. Japan had accumulated its many thousands of American wards in its empire, while America's only high-value bargaining material consisted of Japanese embassy and consular personnel. Otherwise, America had Japanese immigrants, such as Miwa and his cohorts at Lordsburg, and Japanese Americans, who were of little or no value to Japan.[17]

The first exchange of prisoners, with both sides earnestly negotiating, was concluded quickly. In addition to Japan's diplomats, it consisted of Japanese journalists, business people, and educators.

In Japan, one of those released from Sugamo Prison in Tokyo was an Associated Press reporter named Max Hill. His jailer told him the same thing that American jailers were telling the Issei: "We have had nothing against you as individuals. But you were enemy aliens. It was necessary to confine you here."[18] Already Japan's resources were stretched thin. Hill and his companions rode to the pier in Yokohama on a bus powered by a charcoal burner. An initial five hundred or so people were loaded at Yokohama, including Ambassador Grew and the embassy staff. About three hundred more prisoners were picked up in Hong Kong and two hundred more were picked up in what then was Saigon (now Ho Chi Minh City, Vietnam).[19] At Singapore, they were joined by a second ship, which carried another six hundred prisoners.

On the American end, an initial thousand prisoners were loaded at New York on a leased Swedish ship, the MS *Gripsholm*. The *Gripsholm* sailed south to Rio de Janeiro, where it picked up four hundred more people, many of them from Japan's embassy in Brazil. The Japanese of Brazil were allowed to carry a large portrait of the emperor aboard, so long as it remained covered in black. They kneeled at the dock and bowed to the black rectangle.

From Rio de Janeiro, the *Gripsholm* crossed the South Atlantic Ocean and went around the south tip of Africa. The exchange occurred at a neutral port on Africa's southeast coast, Lourenço Marques, in the Portuguese colony of Mozambique, facing the island of Madagascar and the Indian Ocean. As this first exchange of civilians was in motion, summer gave way to winter at Lordsburg, and the Lordsburg prisoners more loudly debated the possibility of returning to Japan by way of a second exchange.

THERE WAS LESS AND LESS FOR the Issei nationalists to cheer about. Japan's startling advances had been stopped. After the Japanese navy was defeated at Midway Island, the tide of war began to shift in America's favor. Miwa's fellow internee, Furuya, described a rumored "Group that Supports the 100-Year War" forming in Japan, weighted against a more optimistic "Group that Supports the Twenty-Five-Year War." Furuya reasoned that even if the war lasted only twenty-five years, "the elderly would be fated to die behind barbed wire."[20] With such a view of reality, interest in repatriation was widespread.

While the pro-Japan element in the Lordsburg camp discussed such notions, for the more rationally inclined, such as Miwa, the belief that Japan's indomitable spirit would prevail was delusional.

Miwa was a man of action who had made money, traveled widely, and gained the respect of both the Japanese community and the multiracial community of Hawai'i. With internment, he had been forced into slow motion. Life in the Lordsburg camp revolved around undemanding tasks, such as representing the men in his barracks. His family was a world away, and news of the war was increasingly bleak. From a savings account at the Bishop National Bank in Honolulu, he was supporting his stepmother, age sixty-seven; his wife, age thirty-eight; daughter Katherine, eighteen; son Shozo, sixteen; and the eleven-year-old Fumio (Lawrence). All of his loved ones were stuck in Japan in what Seigo accurately discerned, through the fog of conflicting propaganda, as a worsening situation.

For Miwa, returning to Hiroshima became a matter of responsibility. When the camp administration asked who would like to be sent to Japan in a second prisoner exchange, Miwa said he would.

On January 7, 1943, twenty-seven months after leaving his family behind in Japan, he signed a form required by the commanding officer of Lordsburg. It acknowledged that "my repatriation has been requested by the Japanese Government, and that I desire to be repatriated when and if facilities become available." He further acknowledged that an exchange might never occur and, even if it did, he might not be chosen to be a part of it.

As the form indicated, a second exchange was uncertain. Following the first exchange, Japanese agents had interviewed the repatriates as to how they had been treated in America. Through the line of communication that ran from Tokyo to the embassy of Spain to the embassy of Switzerland, Japan berated the American government for its treatment of Japanese diplomats, Japanese aliens, and Japanese Americans.

Japan objected to the Honolulu police taking control of the consulate on December 7 and to the Japanese consul being strip-searched. It objected to the women of the Honolulu consulate being disrobed down to their "chemise," and to security personnel pawing through their lacquered hair, searching for hidden objects. It objected to repeated searches of their luggage. It reminded Americans that one of its security agents had cut open a child's teddy bear, looking for contraband. It quibbled over the disappearance of sixty dollars and two baseball gloves.[21]

Obviously, the Japanese government had learned the details of

Sand Island. It protested the old men standing naked in formation in the cold rain, as well as the continuation of security arrests throughout Hawai'i in the months after the bombing.

The Special Division of the U.S. State Department promised to investigate Japan's charges. It acknowledged that some were accurate, such as the police takeover of the Honolulu consulate and the military formation of the aged. It dismissed other charges as routine procedures to which everyone was subjected, such as the search of luggage.

America went to great lengths pursuing a second exchange with Japan, all but groveling in its secret communications. However, for public consumption the U.S. government could not resist the propaganda possibilities of the first exchange. An American businessman, rescued from Shanghai, announced in a newsreel that Japan was beaten, and that it was searching for an exit from the war. The correspondent Max Hill's book, published only weeks after his return, said Japan must be destroyed "with methods as ruthless as their own or suffer a bondage worse than that endured by the Jews in Egypt."[22]

Reaching for moral high ground, the American government announced that no one would be sent to Japan against his or her will. With this nominally humanitarian limitation, the Special Division searched for a shipful of potential repatriates who would be sufficiently attractive to Japan to bring about another exchange. Through surveys of the one hundred and twenty thousand people driven out of the West Coast, it became apparent that in fact most did not want to go to Japan, even if it meant getting out of what were, for all practical purposes, prison camps. Two-thirds of the occupants of the so-called "internment camps" were American born, and therefore American citizens, and for them there was no such thing as "going home" or "going back."

The search for exchanges was complicated by the fact that, at least in theory, only persons specifically named by Japan could be repatriated, as James Miwa had been arbitrarily prompted to state in the form he signed. At a meeting between internees and the Spanish consul at the Missoula, Montana, camp, a prisoner asked the consul, "Was the list of repatriates made by the Japanese government?" The answer was an unequivocal yes.[23]

The Spanish consul also was asked, "Why were some internees forced to repatriate against their will?" Two names were recited, both Japanese from Latin American countries. The consul passed the question to the camp administrator, who continued to blame Japan by saying, "The Japanese government makes the selection by itself."[24]

The consul also was asked why some potential repatriates from Hawai'i were not allowed to bring their families with them, and why they were in fact "forced to sign an agreement indicating their desire to repatriate alone." For this there was no answer.

Contrary to its professed policy, the American government forced an unacknowledged number of people into repatriation. One such person, named Yoshiro Shibata, was eventually to sue for reinstatement of his U.S. citizenship in the Federal District Court of Southern California, claiming that he had been forced to go to Japan (and also that subsequently he had been impressed into the army of Japan against his will). The Court found in his favor, and his American citizenship was restored.[25]

Camps such as Miwa's—the camps holding influential Japanese immigrants who had been rounded up by the FBI—were high-percentage places to troll for prisoners who actually wanted to be repatriated. While pressure undoubtedly was applied in certain cases, most of the people who asked for repatriation appear to have done so voluntarily.

Motivations varied. Some who nursed hurt feelings looked to Japan for healing. A certain Mr. T. of Hawai'i Island possessed a nail that he took with him to Lordsburg from Sand Island. Lacking other means, he used it to clean his ear. When the nail was discovered, he was subjected to a mock court proceeding on the charge of possessing a weapon. Fellow inmates were forced to act as jurors. Others were ordered to serve as prosecutors. Mr. T. was forced to apologize. The presiding officer found him guilty based on his apology and fined him to forfeit his next ration of cigarettes and candy. Mr. T. repatriated, often recounting that he had never felt more humiliated than at the trial before his fellow internees.

Although Lordsburg played a significant role in the second prisoner exchange, the largest single element was from a uniquely sinister camp run by the U.S. Immigration and Naturalization Service at Crystal City, Texas. Early in the war, Latin American governments had rounded up their more successful and prominent residents of Japanese ancestry, including citizens. This was done with not only the encouragement of the American government but the active involvement of the FBI, whose agents swarmed through Latin American countries by the hundreds. Most of the Latin Americans of Japanese ancestry had migrated after 1907, the year of the San Francisco school segregation crisis, or after 1924, when the U.S. Congress had closed the door on Japanese immigration. They often spoke Spanish or Portuguese and had first names derived from their adopted cultures. In 1942, many were snatched off the street by security agents. They disappeared into the dragnet. Particularly large numbers were taken from Peru, and others from Brazil, El Salvador, and Ecuador.

In captivity, they were aggregated in a prison camp in the American-controlled Panama Canal Zone. From there they were shipped to New Orleans, sprayed with disinfectant, then shipped by train to San Antonio, Texas. From San Antonio they were transported by bus to the Crystal City camp.

If the forced relocation and incarceration of 120,000 Japanese Americans and Japanese aliens was to be the darkest internal-security episode of America's history, as would be eventually argued long after the fact, the treatment of the Latin Americans by the U.S. government was a black hole. The weather in south Texas was hot, dust was everywhere, and nothing quite grew like the cockleburs. For cosmetic purposes, the American government made a propaganda film about the livability of Crystal City, featuring paradoxical touches, including a large swimming pool. It was sometimes referred to as "Family Camp."

Meanwhile, the Lordsburg camp was vacated by the army to make room for enemy soldiers who had been taken in combat as prisoners of war. Miwa and his fellows from Hawai'i were moved north to Santa Fe, a less harsh environment. Nearly eight hundred Hawai'i internees converged in Santa Fe from various camps, such as Missoula, Montana, and Livingston, Louisiana, creating a buzz of excitement and a sharing of internment stories. However, Issei from the U.S. mainland and Latin America soon outnumbered the Hawai'i contingent.[26] The rancorous debate over who was winning the war intensified, and the potential repatriates waited anxiously to see if there would be a second prisoner exchange.

WHILE MIWA WAITED, HE WROTE A painful letter to the former U.S. ambassador to Japan, Joseph Grew, dated March 29, 1943. Miwa said he wanted to return to Japan at his own expense via neutral countries to work as an interpreter among American internees. In essence, he was offering to give up the relative comfort of Lordsburg for far worse conditions in the internment camps of Japan. He added his willingness to go "elsewhere in the Orient."

He said that having been educated in the United States and having lived in Honolulu from 1914 to 1934, "I believe that is my obligation to do so." He asked Grew for help. By way of introduction, Miwa wrote that he had a close friend in Hiroshima who was related to a man who had worked for Grew in Tokyo. He said he had paid fourteen thousand dollars in taxes to the U.S. government the preceding year. He described how his passport had expired due to circumstances beyond his control, suggesting but not quite saying that his internment had resulted from a passport problem.

On the face of it, the idea of repatriating and working as an interpreter among the American internees may have seemed farfetched or quixotic. Only later, as events unfolded, would it become apparent that it contained the elements of Miwa's plan for how to get himself and his family through the war. His return to Japan was only the first step. He was ready to accept that Japan would lose the war and that he could regroup with his family by putting his knowledge of the two countries to work.

Grew treated Seigo's letter with concern but apparently did not know what to make of it. He quickly passed it on to the Passport Division and then the Special Division of the State Department, asking what he should say in reply. The letter was fielded by a General B. M. Bryan, director of the Aliens Division of the Office of the Provost Marshal General of the War Department, who then routed it to the assistant chief of the Special Division. The Special Division confused the issue by replying that "the question of his possible repatriation" should be taken up with the intermediaries of the Spanish Embassy. General Bryan then wrote to the commander of the Lordsburg camp, saying that Miwa's questions about repatriation should be routed to the Spanish Embassy. There the idea hit a dead end.

Meanwhile, negotiation of a second exchange lurched from problem to problem. Japan sent a list of four thousand names of people it wanted, but many on Japan's list did not want to be repatriated. The United States said it could locate only 580 of the people on Japan's list. Japan insisted that the United States look harder, which it did, miraculously locating another 2,400 in the next six weeks.

How many, if any, might be exchanged from the large Japanese community in Hawai'i was in question. While 248 internees from Hawai'i by then had asked for repatriation, both the navy and the army objected on security grounds to anyone from Hawai'i being exchanged.[27] The martial law governor of Hawai'i, Delos C. Emmons, opposed anyone returning to Japan because, he argued, such persons could supply Japan with strategic information about the islands.

In reality, strategic information about defenses in Hawai'i was in plain view from many angles, as the Pearl Harbor attack had proven. More likely Emmons's objection reflected his opposition to any sort of further relocation of Hawai'i's Japanese community. Emmons was determined to bolster community morale by expanding participation in the U.S. war effort, and shipping people to Japan was, in those terms, counterproductive.

Other issues surrounded the Hawai'i applications for reparation. For the FBI, which had the most direct control of internal security, director J. Edgar Hoover objected to the repatriation of consular agents, priests, and fishermen—in other words, to the categories of internees who had made up the majority of the December 7 FBI sweep in the first place.[28]

Weighted against the security objections coming from Hawai'i was the imperative of getting as many Americans out of Japan's hands as possible. In the beginning months of the war, Japan had allowed a number of Americans to continue living and sometimes working in place under surveillance. It was America, not Japan, that had planned an internal security sweep prior to the actual fighting. In that light, according to one line of thought, Japan's internment program was a response to America's internment program, and in particular it was a response to the massive removal and forced relocation from the West Coast states. In any event, as the war progressed, and as Japan's fortunes declined, reports of Japan's camps became progressively dire. American prisoners were being subjected to brutal treatment, starving, and dying.

With a painful slowness, details of a second exchange were worked out in August 1943, more than a year after the first exchange. Miwa was on the list. According to a count by the Hawai'i internee Sukei Furuya, seventy-one were from Hawai'i, including a number of wives and children.[29] Along with a sizable contingent of the Lordsburg internees by then in Santa Fe, Miwa was transported by train to New York City.

THE U.S. GOVERNMENT AGAIN CHARTERED THE MS *Gripsholm*. The ship, owned by a Swedish company, was first-rate, if aging. Built in 1925 in England, it was the first diesel-powered liner in the Atlantic service, foreshadowing the displacement of steam-powered ships by diesel-powered ships.

The *Gripsholm* was built for fifteen hundred passengers, which is apparently why that had become the magic number on the scales of the exchange. Actually, there were 1,340 passengers on the boarding list, which meant there was ample room for all. More than half were ethnic Japanese from Latin American countries.[30]

The *Gripsholm* was loaded on the New Jersey side of New York Harbor on September 1, 1943. The U.S. government photographed the passengers in great detail. In all, 274 photographs were taken. The most likely purpose was to provide reassurance to Japan that its nationals were being well cared for. Dozens of photographs showed people as they debarked from trains, as they boarded buses for the dock, as their baggage was checked at dockside, as they boarded, and as they strolled about their new luxury liner. There were sixteen views of the ship's interior, ten views of passengers enjoying the accommodations, and six of food for their first meal aboard, which consisted of a Swedish smorgasbord, filet mignon, and honeydew melon.

Everyone was well dressed and often smiling. The excitement of many of the passengers was palpable. A family with two small girls and a little boy, dressed in fine clothes, appeared in several of the photos. Other photos were less convincing. Old men sat glumly on wooden benches, leaning against walking sticks, under the watchful eye of U.S. military personnel. Some of the people were alarmingly thin, as if they had not been eating well.

Passenger service on the outbound voyage was comparable to peacetime service. The bar and lounges were open and stocked with liquor, wine, and beer. There were three different theaters, which showed American movies. One was *Yankee Doodle Dandy.* Each person was allowed to take three hundred dollars out of the country, as well as three suitcases.[31]

THE *GRIPSHOLM* SAILED ON SEPTEMBER 2, 1943, passing the Statue of Liberty, which famously urged the passerby, "Give me your tired, your poor, your huddled masses yearning to breathe free." The question of how to immunize a ship at sea from attack haunted the undertaking. At first Japan wanted the exchange ship to be portrayed as a hospital ship but then agreed to have it painted with the word "diplomat."

At night the ship was fully lighted so that friend and foe alike could read the word DIPLOMAT, which was rendered in enormous letters on the side of the ship. Friendly ships passing in the night raced away from the *Gripsholm* at top speed, so as not to create a silhouetted target against the *Gripsholm's* lights.

Issei men who previously had crossed from Hawai'i to San Francisco locked in stinking rooms, urinating into tin cans, now strolled

The gaiety and well-being of these departing passengers, captured here, conveyed the U.S. desire to reassure Japan that Japanese aliens and Japanese Americans were well cared for. The goal was a continued prisoner exchange. (Courtesy of U.S. National Archives)

the deck of the *Gripsholm*. They chatted by the rail and watched movies. Some attended classes in language and culture, taught by onboard *sensei*.

The ship sailed around the southern tip of Africa without incident. Symptomatic of Japan's situational leverage, the Japanese government

Older male prisoners, under armed guard awaiting departure, conveyed a contrary mood. (Courtesy of U.S. National Archives)

The MS *Gripsholm* under way, painted with the word DIPLOMAT for purposes of safe passage.

insisted on moving the exchange point from Mozambique in East Africa to the Portuguese colony of Goa on the west coast of India. This added the Indian Ocean to the *Gripsholm*'s travel distance. The United States acceded.

At Goa, the *Gripsholm* and the Japanese ship were docked alongside one another. The passengers disembarked from the bow of the *Gripsholm* into the bow of Japan's ship, while the prisoners of Japan disembarked from stern to stern. The *Gripsholm* staff greeted the freed Americans with a lavish buffet. At the sight of so much food, many of the passengers—some on the edge of starving to death—sank to their knees in prayer. Members of the Swedish crew wept.

Japan's ship had been pilfered from France as booty of war. In its prior life it was named the MS *Aramis,* a ship of the French colonial fleet in Southeast Asia, then known as French Indochina. Britain had tried desperately to keep the French fleet under Allied control, but it had slipped away from the Allies through the auspices of the Vichy France government, which had collaborated with the German invaders of France. Through Vichy, Japan put the *Aramis* to work for the Axis. The French crew was dropped ashore in Vietnam. The Japanese quickly mastered operation of the vessel, renaming it the *Teia Maru.* It was built for a thousand passengers, two-thirds the capacity of the *Gripsholm.*

The poor condition of the *Teia Maru* strengthened Seigo's perception of how the war was going for Japan. Mothers and young children were assigned to cabins, but others slept in makeshift shelters on the deck. One of the families was that of Shoichi Asami, the managing editor of the *Hawaii Times.* Asami had written from a mainland camp that he wanted his family to go to Japan. To the later regret of his oldest son, Kinichi, the family did not object. After a year of being shuffled among camps, they had been reunited in May 1943 in Crystal City. Daughter Jane Asami was sixteen at the time. She remembered the food on the *Teia Maru* as worse than terrible: "I remember worms floating in the rice." Because of overcrowding, passengers often stood in long queues. "I can still remember a pregnant woman, nearly ready to give birth. She, too, had to stand in line even to use the toilet. It was pathetic."[32]

At Singapore, which was occupied by Japan, the passengers were given a tour of the city. They encountered Japanese officers wearing long swords as well as soldiers carrying their guns with fixed bayonets, making their weapons longer than the average soldier was tall. The Japanese officers boasted of how they had taken Singapore by land, while the fearsome British cannons still pointed toward the sea.

Japanese officials recruited passengers to stay on in Singapore and do the work of this newly acquired piece of the empire. Twenty families did so, including the Asami family. Jane was assigned to monitor wiretaps on suspected pro-American or pro-British residents, a job she performed reluctantly. Brother Kinichi also monitored wiretaps but then was drafted into the Japanese army, where he was made to feel he lacked the samurai spirit of *bushidō*. The family patriarch wrote newspaper dispatches that fed Japan's war machine. Now and then someone would ask them about their prior life in Hawai'i.[33]

Seigo Miwa, as part of the large majority of passengers, continued on from Singapore. The next stop was Manila. Passengers were given stalks of green bananas and told to eat them as the bananas ripened. A little Japanese American boy named Archie Miyamoto remembered that as they voyaged north, the weather grew colder, and the bananas refused to ripen. Like young Jane, little Archie remembered the white worms in the rice. They were not always visible but squished when bitten.[34]

The ship arrived in Yokohama Harbor in December 1943. From the railing, Seigo Miwa could see the deteriorating condition of the country firsthand. The dwindling food supply was strictly rationed. Despite Japan's conquest of the oil fields of Southeast Asia, energy was in painfully short supply. Not only taxicabs but other forms of ground transportation were running on charcoal. If Seigo had not already reached an opinion about the outcome of the war, he did so now. Later he would tell Katherine that as he looked around, he irrevocably concluded that Japan was beaten. The details of surrender were, in his mind, only a matter of time.

He caught a train for Hiroshima and disembarked at the Yokogawa Station. From there it was a walk of only several blocks down Miwa Street to his home.

PART III
In Japan

CHAPTER SIX

Coming of Age in Hiroshima

By being born in Honolulu in the predawn of July 5, 1931, Larry Miwa missed the celebration of the Fourth of July by a few hours. As a grim reminder of infant mortality, his birth certificate asked for the number of children in his family "born alive and now living." The answer was three. For the question "Born alive but now dead," the answer was one, which tended to explain the five- and eight-year age gaps between Larry and his older siblings.

Larry was an American citizen by virtue of birth and a citizen of Japan by virtue of registration at the Japanese consulate in Honolulu. Katherine and Shozo previously had been registered, and Seigo Miwa then registered the infant Larry, believing that he was creating options for his children as they grew up.

In his baby picture, Larry is dressed in a white linen gown, which was the style of the period for those who could afford a studio portrait. Coincident with his birth, the United States was falling into the Great Depression, but the Miwa family business seems to have been little affected. If anything, its fortunes were rising. By 1931, J. S. Miwa had become a middleman. In the archaic vocabulary of the Hawaiian economy, he was a "factor," an agent of business who concentrates on buying and selling a wide range of goods. In certain circles, the Miwa name was known as one of the Japanese Big Five. Compared to the haole Big Five, with their control of plantations, banks, trading houses, shipping lines, and the waterfront, a business like Miwa's was small stuff, but it rested solidly on the multiple generations of Japanese who populated Hawai'i. Despite the Depression, the J. S. Miwa store maintained its fleet of twenty-three delivery trucks, which put the company in a remarkably good position, since most of its customers did not yet own motor vehicles. In addition to the main operation in Kalihi, there

Lawrence Fumio Miwa, son of James Seigo Miwa, infant portrait, July 1931. (Miwa Family Collection)

was the Miwa store in the Japanese district of Mō'ili'ili and also the Miwa store in Nu'uanu. Miwa Ltd. imported goods from Osaka as well as Hiroshima, and it also shipped goods into San Francisco.

Like many Japanese in Hawai'i, James was determined to give his three children a base in Japanese language and culture. In almost every Japanese household, this goal translated into the children's attendance at a Japanese language school in Hawai'i. For others, it meant a visit to Japan, sometimes for a year or two, to unite with grandparents or to care for an aged relative. For Miwa, the plan was more ambitious.

Not long before Larry's birth, James and his wife Yoshio went to Japan on a family vacation, combined with business. Katherine and Shozo went along. Following Larry's birth, Miwa relocated Katherine to Japan and subsequently relocated Shozo as well.

It is a matter of speculation whether racial issues within Hawai'i, as well as events in Asia, were a factor in the monumental decision that Miwa was making. In 1928, the veil of Island good will was pierced by the Fukunaga murder case, in which a deranged young man of Japanese ancestry named Miles Fukunaga kidnapped and murdered the son of a haole family. The event brought down a load of culturally induced shame on people of Japanese ancestry and also a fear of reprisal. Japanese families in Honolulu were known to instruct their children to walk straight home from school and not to go out at night.

In 1932, the tenuous status of Japanese and other nonwhite

people in Hawai'i was thrown into stark relief by a second dramatic crime case in which a U.S. naval officer's wife, Thelma Massie, claimed to have been raped by a gang of young local men. Thelma Massie's husband and her mother-in-law retaliated by kidnapping and murdering one of the accused young men. The Territorial governor—under pressure from the U.S. Navy Department—commuted their sentence for murder to one hour in the governor's office in 'Iolani Palace. Such a blatant miscarriage of justice sent a deadly chill through the local community. The American government had treated Hawai'i as an overseas colony, and all too obviously the rule of law had been trampled by white racism.

When Larry was two years old, before he had developed memory of Hawai'i, Seigo moved him to Japan to be with his mother and two older siblings.

The trans-Pacific practice first established by Marujiro, and followed by Senkichi, now was continued into the life of J. S. Miwa's immediate family. In this, the Miwas were a minority within a minority. About a third of the great wave of Japanese migrants actually had settled in Hawai'i; another large element had moved on to the American continent; and most of the remainder had returned to Japan. Only a small but influential sliver, the Miwas among them, attempted to be an ongoing part of two countries.

LARRY'S FIRST CLEAR MEMORIES OF INFANCY were of his family greeting him at the dock at Yokohama. From the moment he disembarked, he was Fumio, not Larry. His father was Seigo, and Katherine was Kiyoko. From Yokohama, the family rode the train south to Osaka, the thriving industrial city that was second in importance only to Tokyo.

For the next several years James Seigo Miwa concentrated on developing the export operation in Osaka. When his father, Senkichi, died, Seigo moved the family to the big house on Miwa Street in Hiroshima. Although they lived near the headquarters of an entire Japanese Army division, Fumio experienced early childhood as a blissful idyll. He thought of Hiroshima as being much like any other city. It was pleasant and peaceful. Yokogawa was like a small town, a part of it organized around his family's very own street, the thirty Miwa tenants, and the Miwa rental shops. The train line was on the uphill end of his street, and the wide, tranquil Ota River began just at the lower end of the street.

Fumio would remember the neighbors of his early childhood as being happy people. The war on the Asian continent occasionally created news of victory in which, Fumio gathered, most people took a certain nationalistic pride.

The Miwa house in Yokogawa was large by any standard and enormous by Japanese standards. Fumio would estimate it to be ten thousand or so square feet, which meant that a dozen or so ordinary Japanese houses could have fit inside it.

The Miwa house was incongruous not only for its size but for its features. The larger American side had two floors. The first floor was warehouse-like. It was stacked with goods, such as salted fish, rice, and firewood. The second floor had seven rooms, including two large bedrooms, each with three beds. Senkichi had created an office for himself in a library on the second floor that now was Seigo's.

Across a footbridge of twenty or so feet was the Japanese house. The perimeter of the house was a sheltered walkway. It had *shoji* doors made of rice paper, and most of the floor was covered by densely woven *tatami* mats, on which people sat. The largest room was a meeting hall, much in the Japanese aristocratic tradition, accommodating several dozen people. Within the Japanese side were several Western adaptations: a sit-down toilet, which substituted for the traditional squat-down toilet; a refrigerator from America; and a more or less Western-style kitchen.

Most importantly, the house was built around a system of steel beams.

The two swords of the family's samurai past, one long and one short, were displayed on a shelf in the Western side of the house, while the Japanese side had a library, stocked with Japanese translations of books originally written in English, including the recently published *Gone with the Wind*. Music was important—not the music of *koto* and *shamisen* but the classical music of the West. Seigo often listened to his phonograph, which was the only one in the neighborhood, and the tenants in the Miwa rentals would also come inside on occasion and listen as well. Mozart and Beethoven were his mainstays, and Brahms and Haydn were ascendant.

Operation of the household was supported by several servants, including a maid, a cook, and a stable boy.

There were pianos in both of the houses, and all three children were required to practice and take lessons. Otherwise, an increasingly sharp distinction was made between Katherine and the two boys. Katherine was pampered. In her first year back in Japan, she was provided with a personal Japanese language tutor, who came to the house. An *ikebana* instructor came to the house to teach the art of flower arrangement. She attended classes to learn the Japanese way of tea, *chanoyu*. The quality and number of her *kimono* were to become a crucial vignette in the family story. One expensive robe after another was brought into the house for her to try on, and many were purchased and piled up in her wardrobe. If she went out, she typically rode in a taxi.

Where Katherine was enrolled in a private school, Fumio and Shozo were enrolled in the neighborhood public school, which was populated by thousands of students, many of whom were from poor families. They were dressed in the black uniforms and black caps of the Japanese schoolboy, each like the other.

Fumio was small and suffered periodically from a respiratory problem. His mother worried about him. During one two-month stretch of his early childhood, she puréed an apple for him every day as a home remedy. When he was nine, his health again seemed to decline. She had a hen that daily laid an egg, which she cooked for him. Fumio would rush home from school, eat the egg, and rush back to school. Late in elementary school, he stayed home for an extended period. When he began feeling better, he played around the neighborhood on his own. He remembered this as a window into freedom that he most valued in childhood. Finally, a teacher saw him and ordered him back to school. From all of this, Fumio was to believe that an apple a day, the hen, and his mother's devotion had saved his life.

Despite his small stature, he had a knack for fitting in and making friends. He was steadfastly cheerful. He was a mediator. One day, word passed through his school that there was to be a fight between two boys down by the river. The idea was for the combatants to get in a few blows and then to step back before anyone got hurt. Fumio was designated to jump in as if inspired by the moment and shout, "That's enough." He jumped in, shouted, and the fight ended.

Many of the school's children were Korean, and a few were Chinese. Fumio went with his mother through the neighborhood, distributing rice. He particularly would remember his mother giving rice to immigrant Koreans who, in his child's view, were merely poor—having no way of understanding they had been systematically impoverished by Japan's colonization of Korea.

Although Fumio was deeply attached to his mother, he also had a keen appreciation for his father. He thought of Seigo as being a bigger force than Grandfather Senkichi ever had been. In his perception, Seigo

Fumio Lawrence Miwa's Misasa Elementary School class photo, 1943. He is in the second row, fourth from the right. (Miwa Family Collection)

had taken the shell of a store in Honolulu and made it work, generating the cash that had built up the family assets in Japan. Wherever Seigo turned his attention, business thrived. In addition to the rubber factory in Yokogawa, subordinates reported to his father from various points in Hiroshima and Osaka, and likewise from across the ocean. For photographic evidence of success there was the building dominated by the big sign, "J. S. MIWA," on North King Street in Honolulu.

Fumio was aware of his father moving back and forth and being gone for long stretches, but it was not until he was ten that Seigo departed for Hawai'i and seemed to be gone for good. By then, Katherine was approaching adulthood, and Shozo was approaching military age. Japan's war on the Asian continent had taken on a life of its own, resulting in the acquisition of more territories and the consuming of more resources. From Chosen, which was Japan's new name for Korea, and from the puppet state of Manchukuo, the war had spread into China's heartland—the China of Shanghai and Nanking—and also to the British and French colonies in Southeast Asia.

One day in early December of 1941, while Fumio was in the garden of the Japanese house, he heard a radio announcer say that Japan had attacked the American naval base at Pearl Harbor. Japan seemed to him to be unbeatable, a view that reflected what he had been told innumerable times. The war was going on all over. He was unaware of his American citizenship, and there was little distinction to be made among enemy nations.

During this period, Fumio knew virtually nothing about his absent father, not even that his father had been interned by the American government. Then, in late 1943, his father suddenly reappeared. In family conversation, Seigo put the best face on his internment experience. He said he always had enough to eat, the food was good, and he even was paid for his work, if only a little. The story seems to have been recited for his family's benefit. He had worried about them, and he wanted to be with them, but they need not have worried about him.

Soon after his father's return home, Fumio saw six Japanese military police come into the house and ask his father questions at length. For people who understood the realities of life in wartime Japan, this was in itself a frightening experience. Regular soldiers saluted the military police smartly. Civilians sometimes bowed to the ground in their presence.[1]

Seigo's most obvious problem was that he had lived in America nearly thirty years. He had extensive holdings in Honolulu and a small stake in San Francisco. At a minimum, the police must have wanted to assure themselves that he was not a plant of the American government. More immediately, he had just traveled across the American continent. He had traveled through New York City and been given a firsthand look at New York Harbor. He remained the person who had been interviewed at Fort Shafter in Honolulu. That is, he was honest to his own detriment.

Who did he think would win the war? he was asked.

When FBI agents in Hawai'i had repeatedly posed this question, he had said he didn't know. How could he know? The fact was he really did not have a clue at that time and therefore, logically and honestly, he could not say. If anything, the Japan of early 1942 was ascendant.

Now a different set of interrogators demanded to know, who did he think would win the war?

Miwa had seen too much, and his proclivity for answering honestly got the best of him. He said he thought America would win.

For the military police, whose duty it was to control people's thoughts, his answer was treasonous. How could Seigo Miwa think such a thing? What had he seen in America that might lead to such a heretical opinion? Belief in Japan's invincibility was an article of faith. Japan had never lost a war; it could not lose, and it would never surrender. Japan would prevail in the great war so long as its people kept their spirits high. To question the inevitability of victory was to question state authority, of which the military police were the dreaded enforcers.

Despite the dangers inherent in his opinion, Seigo continued for a time to express his views around home. One on one, Seigo told Fumio, "You don't know this, because you are a young boy, but I don't think Japan is going to win." Fumio remembered saying, "Okay, Father. That's what you believe. But in our school class, we believe otherwise." If Fumio were to internalize his father's views, he and the entire family might have come to the attention of his fellow students and his teachers.

Having moved to Hiroshima as an infant, Fumio knew nothing other than Japan. The Japanese government created norms and prescribed behaviors that one did not question. "This is the way things are," he was to recall. "This is the way our lives should be led." He did not regard Japanese society as repressive, but merely as a standard-bearer of how and why to worship the emperor. Everyone accepted that they must be ready to die for the country. It was the way of things. It was the long reach of Great Grandfather Marujiro's time, when the value placed on loyalty was elevated to the pinnacle of the elaborate pyramid of Japanese values.

Katherine differed. Her additional eight years of life and memories of Hawai'i had given her a space for harboring a contrary viewpoint. She regarded the emperor with distaste and thought of the war as folly. America was, in her mind, the country with every imaginable resource, and it was crazy for Japan to engage such a country in war.

Their mother, Yoshio, responded with the pragmatism of someone bent, above all, on her family's survival. She became vehement in her own view that, under the circumstances, Seigo was not to again express his opinion about which country would win. She told her husband to never again talk about Japan losing the war, and he fell silent.

Seigo was questioned repeatedly by the military police. When he went for a walk, they shadowed him. He became isolated. Once an active conversationalist, Seigo now had no story to tell. He did not talk further about internment. He never talked about the prisoner exchange, nor of his circumnavigation of the globe, nor even of Hawai'i. Only Japan regarded him as its citizen, but he had become an odd man out. Eventually, the police lost interest.

Seigo played his records on the family phonograph. He spent hours playing cards by himself, a form of solo trumps. Fumio would remember his father alone in a small room on the Japanese side of the bifurcated house, facing the garden. Sometimes his obsession with cards went on from morning until night.

Because of his prolonged absence from Japan, and also because of his shaky position, Seigo's role in the Miwa businesses was over. Young Fumio inferred that his father had done well in Hawai'i only because the family's refrigerator was from Honolulu. Fumio's understanding was that the family lived off the rental units that Senkichi had built. Their income was curtailed, but they were still better off than most people.

OTHERWISE, FUMIO REMEMBERED HIS FIFTH-GRADE YEAR in elementary school for two things. One was that, despite pressures for him to toughen up, his mother continued to demand that he take piano lessons. When the school held a piano recital, it was with great reluctance and minimal skill that he played Mozart's "Turkish March." He was mortified.

Second, he wondered why his parents didn't send him to a nicer school, given their comparatively privileged status. One day, the principal called him out from the public school's thousands of students, along with two other boys, to take a test for an elite middle school nearby. It was a feeder to Fuzoku High School, which in turn was affiliated with Fuzoku Teachers' College.

The test was divided into six parts. Fumio scored one hundred on five of the six parts. On the final part he scored ninety-eight. When he asked about the two points, the teacher replied that Fumio had correctly given the textbook answer but that he expected a little more from such a good student. Fumio and one other boy were admitted to Fuzoku, but the third boy was declined, a fate that would prove fatal.

The *Fuzoku Chugakko* was within walking distance of the Miwa house. It was located across the Yokogawa Bridge, past the domed Building of Industry and Commerce, by the next bend in the river.

It had sixth, seventh, and eighth grades. Fumio would remember his elementary schooling as providing a straightforward education, but in contrast his middle school was infused with military propaganda. He now dressed in a paramilitary uniform. *Yamato damashii,* the spirit of Japan; and *bushidō,* the way of the warrior, were school staples. At the core of this construct was veneration of the emperor. In previous centuries, the ancient institution of the emperor had become tarnished. At one point, it appears that a majority of Japanese did not know that an emperor existed. One medieval emperor sold poems in the street for income. Another, on his death, was allowed to lie around for six weeks for lack of funeral arrangements.

For a student such as Fumio in wartime Japan, no such earthbound information existed. The emperor was everywhere portrayed as divine. Children were taught that when it was time for a human male to become an emperor, he crawled into the womb of the sun goddess, Amaterasu, who then gave birth to him as a god. What was passed off as a return to tradition, a Japanese American scholar would come to believe, "was actually based on a fantastic jumble of notions lifted from Marxism, fascism, Nazism, Haushoferian geopolitics, Malthusianism, Confucianism, Shintoism, Pan-Asianism and other widely divergent sources, all pieced together with wild imagination."[2]

Nonetheless, the ideology of Japan attained an enormous power over people's minds. At its zenith, most people went along. Certainly schoolchildren went along.[3] General Hideki Tojo had decreed to Japan's fighting men that they must "Never live to experience shame as a prisoner."[4] High-ranking officers who faced defeat in battle were expected to kill themselves, leaving men in the lower ranks to lead the ordinary soldier—wounded, starving, or ill—in desperation charges that amounted to mass suicide.[5] In those rare instances where someone survived, families were not told that their loved ones, to their shame, were still alive. The more perilous Japan's real military position, the harsher the practices became, and the louder the drum of propaganda beat.[6]

Rational people such as Seigo were regarded as being of a lower moral order, valuing materialistic measures such as personal wealth, commerce, and industrial output. Incrementally, the Miwas drifted from a position of influence toward the margins. Army personnel came around to the Miwa house, announcing they were going to use it as sleeping quarters for officers, which they did. Fumio assumed this practice was going on everywhere, so he did not think this was particularly strange. The officers took over the majority of the living space. The family squeezed into several of the smaller rooms and also moved part of their belongings into one of the rentals. They barely spoke to the officers, and the officers did not speak to them.

Katherine had gone away to school in Kobe, but suddenly Kobe was under siege from the air. Deadly bombs started fires that in turn created firestorms. With a sense of bitterness, Katherine observed that the firefighting plan of last resort was a government order for each family to keep a full tub of water in their front yard. She was badly frightened by the incessant raids, and her family was frightened for her. They told her to return to Hiroshima.

The scourge of the American firebombing spread to over sixty Japanese cities, but Hiroshima was eerily exempt. Then one particular day, an American reconnaissance plane lumbered over at high altitude. From the perspective of the ground, nothing happened. Actually, the airplane's crew was taking "before" photographs. The flyover yielded detailed images of a thriving, well-organized metropolis by the sea, laid out around its multiple rivers, with clouds drifting gently here and there in the summer sky.

Although Hiroshima was important militarily, it had not been subjected to conventional bombing for a particular reason: it was on the short list of the U.S. government's potential targets for the first atomic bomb strike. The United States was interested in a clean laboratory. If such a momentous experiment were to be made, American war strategists wanted to compare the effects of conventional bombing and atomic bombing.

The aerial photographs revealed that the city of Hiroshima anticipated bombing of the scale and type that had been carried out upon

U.S. Army air reconnaissance of Hiroshima, Japan, prior to the August 6, 1945, atomic bombing. (Courtesy of Hiroshima Peace Memorial Museum, originally from U.S. National Archives)

other Japanese cities. The evidence lay in the city's creation of fire-breaks. Within a firebreak zone, man-made construction was torn out and combustible material was removed. Tens of thousands of people were mobilized for this work, including thousands of schoolchildren.

The Miwa family was all too aware of the firebreak strategy, because some of their buildings had been leveled on the uphill side of Miwa Street in the direction of Yokogawa Station. If making such choices was inherently difficult for a civil defense official, the choice to level Miwa's buildings had likely been made easier by Seigo Miwa's being in disrepute with the authorities.

In addition to observing the firebreaks, American intelligence analysts might also have noticed that throughout the city a number of people were being evacuated.

On July 3, 1945, two days before Fumio's fourteenth birthday, he was told by school officials to pack a light bag, because he and his classmates were moving to the countryside to serve the emperor by growing vegetables. The precipitous nature of the move, as well as the veil of patriotic labor, obscured the purpose of evacuation. That Fumio and the other students might be part of an exodus in expectation of bombing did not occur to their young minds. They were going to grow food and help their beloved country.

They wanted to win the war, but nonetheless they felt the pangs of separation from their parents. They were seventh graders.

CHAPTER SEVEN

A Schoolboy's Diary

On the first day of the evacuation, the teacher instructed the boys to keep what he called a self-reflection diary. As a fragment of national history, such a diary created a record of the dogma of militarized Japan as it played out among middle school students. In the practice of making diary entries, Fumio's sense of self-awareness grew, and he increasingly recorded his personal experiences and emotions.

On July 4, the day after receiving notice to pack up, his first sentence was "Objective: We should not die in vain by the enemy bombs so that we can devote ourselves to the country."

He and his classmates boarded a train at Hiroshima Station at 9:29 a.m., riding through "beautiful and lush countryside scenery" to a place called Kochi Station, disembarking about 11:30 a.m. They loaded their bags on a truck and then walked six miles to a village called Tonomura, where they occupied an elementary school dormitory. They were about twenty-five miles east of downtown Hiroshima.

That evening the dormitory chief lectured them on dos and don'ts. "Take meals with appreciation. Avoid getting a chill while sleeping. Hand towels should be hung on the ropes and keep your belongings organized. Slippers should be kept on the shoe racks." And so on. Fumio determined to follow all instructions. He went to bed and fell asleep, only to be awakened by the teacher, a Mr. Nakamura, who announced that the truck had arrived with their baggage. Everyone turned out to unload the truck, working for an hour in high spirits. Fumio wrote that he was no longer tired, but that Mr. Nakamura was exhausted.

The next day the class stocked up on soybean paste, rice, and firewood. In the evening, the students listened to a discussion of ethics by the dormitory chief.

Particularly in the beginning of the daily entries, a student first wrote down an approximation of what was said by the teacher, who was young and aggressive, essentially a voice of the military regime. His authority was absolute, and nobody questioned him, let alone debated him.

On the first full day in camp, the students dug weeds in an upland area to clear a farm plot, which was divided into small patches. Within a patch, a pair of students was responsible for such items as eggplant, sweet potatoes, and burdock. "I felt I was in line with the national goal to grow more produce," Fumio wrote.

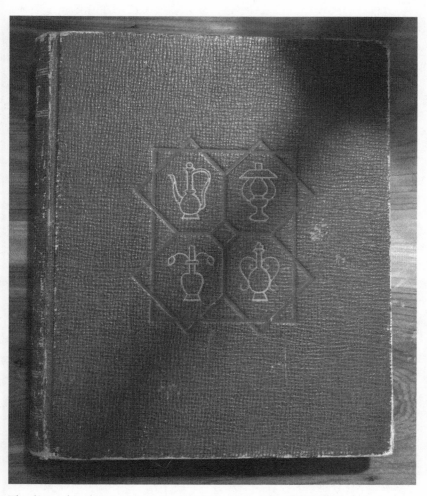

The diary of student Lawrence Fumio Miwa. (Miwa Family Collection)

A daily routine was established. The dormitory chief woke the boys at 5:40 a.m., giving them a few minutes for grooming themselves and cleaning their bunk areas. At 6:00 they turned out to a shrine that was the centerpiece of the school. It housed a photograph of Emperor Hirohito and Empress Nagako, along with various statements by the emperor about the waging of war. The students bowed to the emperor and recited the Emperor's Imperial Rescript on service to the nation in wartime. They sent greetings to their parents, listened to the daily instruction of the dormitory chief, and performed calisthenics.

At breakfast, the boys engaged in silent prayer during which they were instructed to again recite key provisions of the Emperor's Imperial Rescript. They worked in the field from 7:00 a.m. until noon, at which time they were to again pray silently by reviewing the words of the emperor. They then worked another four and one-half hours. At 6:00 p.m. they reassembled at the emperor's shrine, prayed, and recited. They bathed and then ate dinner, during which they were again instructed to silently pray by reciting the Rescript. They were to engage in "private study" from 7:00 to 9:00 p.m. and turn lights out at 9:30, reciting words of acknowledgment and tribute to their teachers and parents.

All in all, they attended two sessions daily of prayerful worship of the emperor and were directed to engage in three more such sessions on their own. They labored in the vegetable enterprise for nine and a half hours, performed calisthenics morning and evening, and studied for two hours, while keeping themselves and their living spaces clean and well organized.

Fumio found school camp life exciting, but he also longed for his parents, particularly for the warmth of his mother. He was at this point four feet, eight inches tall. At his age he might have begun growing more rapidly, but he now had less to eat, and his growth stalled.

The daily work of creating a small farm out of an unfarmed mountainside was no small task. Fumio's assigned area grew a dwarf bamboo, which covered more than half of his patch. "Cutting the bamboo grass properly was difficult," Fumio wrote in his diary. "I tried to find the best way to do it but was unsuccessful." Nonetheless, after cutting bamboo, he and his classmates planted sweet potato vines. The next day he planted ten eggplant seedlings, each in its own hole, following the instructions of his teacher. He was learning a new respect for farmers, estimating that to be a first-rate farmer he would have to practice for ten years.

On a break from their labors, the teacher explained the importance of deeds over words. They worked on until 6:00 p.m. in high spirits. The teacher praised them as having transcended words. They were performing deeds. The next day Fumio planted twenty-six eggplants, anxiously hopeful that they would mature and bear fruit.

His young mind was filled with thoughts of war and vegetables. Late in life, he would think of these as dichotomous. Growing things had to do with creating and sustaining, while war had to do with death and destruction. A teacher from the Agricultural Association instructed them on a simple integration of the two, which Fumio duly recorded as "Vegetables need to be tended with loving care. That is also true of our imperial homeland." Whenever he recalled this particular line, he resolved anew to take good care of his plants.

At dinner on the day of Fumio's planting twenty-six eggplants, the teacher announced that the boys would receive two-day weekend passes on a rotating basis to visit home. The teacher gave out guidelines for home visits that in their detail rivaled the first day's guidelines for camp life: "Work in teams of three to meet at and leave Hiroshima Station." "Act prudently, always bearing in mind that you have an image to uphold." "(If) you encounter air attacks while in Hiroshima City, act quickly and efficiently," et cetera.

The next day, the first team of three boys departed. "(They) left to visit their parents in our dear hometown in Hiroshima," Fumio wrote. "I wish I were going too, I thought as I returned to school."

On July 11, a teacher from the school's Hiroshima campus arrived at the camp. He announced that two-thirds of the school now had been evacuated, although there had been no air raids on the city. Fumio was grateful that the teacher had cared enough to come.

July 12: "Japan is in a state of emergency and now is the time for us and the country to show the world our virtues," Fumio wrote. "If we do this, I am convinced our enemies would not dare to invade our homeland, the great Empire of Japan."

July 13: Two more teams of three students were called out to rotate into Hiroshima. They ate hurriedly and left rice on their plates. Fumio ate part of the leftovers. "While washing the dishes, I thought of my dear mother."

The students switched from developing the gardens midway up the mountain to developing a waterway near the top. Digging was even harder work than clearing and weeding, but the environment was serene. "Surrounded by the mountains, it is a very quiet place where clear water gushes forth from the reservoir," Fumio wrote. "It is a healthy place to be working." They climbed a cliff, tearing dirt from the mountainside and heaping it below them. "I felt I should put my heart and soul into my work, just as the teacher had instructed."

Back in camp, they were treated to a movie version of *Chūshingura*—the classic story of the forty-seven warriors that had been so well attended by his father's peers at the Lordsburg camp in New Mexico.

Fumio particularly liked a second feature, *"Mother Fights for Her Son,"* the story of a widow who scrapes to raise her children and eventually sends a son off to become an officer in the Imperial Navy. Fumio was alive with thoughts of his own mother. "To think that mothers would do anything for the sake of their children. They are more than we deserve." He was told that he would soon get a two-day pass home. "My heart danced," he wrote.

July 17: Returning to his home in Hiroshima, he greeted his parents with a ritual word of good cheer: *Tadaima!* "I am home." After talking with them at great length, he read newspapers for the first time in a long while. "I learned that the war situation was turning for the worse," he wrote. This led him to think that students had to approach their work even more diligently. He wanted to talk with his parents about the war news, but he was interrupted by an air raid alert, which turned out to be a false alarm. He went to bed and slept for nine hours.

July 18: "I felt great." His mother cooked him eggs for breakfast. His father baked a loaf of bread, then asked him numerous questions about his daily routine at camp. "I recounted many pleasant episodes and experiences," Fumio wrote. Katherine was now home from the devastation of Kobe. She went to the train station and bought his return ticket. His brother Shozo, now in the Japanese army, was the subject of a solemn conversation with his mother, who concluded, "You should do your best, just like your brother does."

He walked from his house in Yokogawa along the Ota River to his school, where he took note that a new vegetable garden had been planted. The plants were bearing little green tomatoes.

July 19 was his day to return to school. "Worried that my baggage was too heavy for me, Mother carried it to the station herself." His two schoolmates were waiting. When he said goodbye to his mother, she again said he should do his best.

Work was rained out at camp, so he turned to a research project on his personal hero, a man named Sakichi Toyoda, who had succeeded in life by inventing an automated loom. A classmate had given Fumio a book about Toyoda, and Fumio had digested it in detail. Toyoda was of Fumio's grandfather's generation. He died in 1930, but by 1937 his company had expanded beyond textiles into the making of motor vehicles, which were being marketed under the trade name Toyota.

Fumio took note of Sakichi Toyoda's humble background, which preceded his success in the industrial city of Nagoya. Fumio was of the opinion that most young men go through a period of self-doubt and often give way to despair, but not his hero Toyoda. "[He] made up his mind not to lose to the Westerners in developing machinery," Fumio wrote. In rainy times, Fumio continued to study the life of Toyoda. He was told to prepare a presentation on the subject, and that with luck an opening for just such an event might occur.

Fumio's teacher left camp for three days to visit his family but posted instructions on how to proceed in his absence. The teacher had become alarmed about water quality. "Do not drink or use water in the river," Fumio wrote. "Drink preheated water if circumstances allow."

Fumio's labor on most days had shifted from the mystery and excitement of gardening to the drudgery of excavating the waterway. The class above Fumio's had arrived in camp, and Fumio's class fell into competing with them in digging on the mountainside: "The dirt flew." They worked perilously near a ledge. Quickly the platform expanded to ten meters by three meters, which Fumio carefully illustrated in his diary. An enormous stone got in the way. Everyone levered the stone with hoe and shovel. After repeated tries, they moved it one meter. The teacher arrived on the scene and exhorted them to greater effort. In the course of the day, they moved the stone seven meters.

The war was never far away. Fumio marched to the mountain worksite with his fellow students singing *"The Song of Tokko-tai,"* which was sung by the pilots who, for the first time, were giving up their lives by flying their airplanes into U.S. Navy vessels at the Battle of Leyte Gulf in the eastern Philippines. It was a mode of attack so lethal that the news of *kamikaze* was initially censored from consumption by the American public.

On some days Fumio could hear the rumble of bombs coming from Yamaguchi Prefecture, to the southwest, but nothing from Hiroshima.

Finally, on July 24, four small airplanes appeared. Fumio mistook their overflight for an attack. "It was so maddening," he wrote, "that I gnashed my teeth in frustration." That night he prayed for the safety of his parents, his brother and sister, and his teacher.

On July 26, a heavy rain opened the opportunity he had hoped for, which was to present his findings on Sakichi Toyoda. He reported to his fellow students that Toyoda's father had been a farmer and a carpenter, from whom Toyoda had learned carpentry. Over his father's objections, he had determined to become an inventor. In this, he had been supported by the instructions of his teacher and the unwavering love of his mother.

Fumio's teacher responded favorably in class and then with written comments in Fumio's diary. He urged Fumio to look to his own life for similarities as well as differences. "[Toyoda] managed to rebound from the many tragedies in his life," the teacher said. "You must immerse yourself in your work with a similar attitude." Perhaps the teacher saw Japan as a tragedy of the moment, when the students did not. "Put your heart and soul into whatever you are doing," the teacher advised, "and forget everything else." Nearly a month had passed since Fumio's abrupt departure from Hiroshima.

August 1, 1945, was an occasion for the boys to reflect and set goals. The teacher listed seven goals, which Fumio wrote down. Leading the list was contemplation of obligation to the emperor.

Fumio again outlined the schedule of the day: Rise with a review of the Imperial Rescript and devotions to the emperor. Work as hard as possible during the day. Engage in self-reflection at night.

Obviously, word was spreading into the camp about a desperate defense of Japan's four home islands. This took the form of a so-called "hundred million" resistance, in which that many people were to be ready to die for Japan. "Our greatest wish is to confront our enemy on our home ground," Fumio wrote.

Fumio paraphrased his teacher by urging everyone to "deepen your friendship with your classmates in the way that soldiers do." Even more important than studying or working was the development of trust. "Become a person who is fully trusted not only by the teacher but by your classmates." They were to give up personal ambition and "focus entirely on meeting the demands of your country." If ever a student acted against "the spirit of group life," he was expected to ask his parents to write a letter removing him from the school. Fumio wrote, "Service, like disservice, reaps its own rewards."

Fumio recorded long passages based on the teacher's words, running on in this vein: "Do not make mistakes or deceive others under any circumstances. Let us be fair and honest."

Given such a vigorous start for August, Fumio was optimistic about the rest of the month: "Our resolve has been strengthened anew."

On the second day of August, he awoke at sunrise in the grip of a dream about his mother and father. In the dream his mother again said, "Do your best, Fumio!" He answered, "Stay well, Mother!" He felt love flowing to him from both of his parents. He then dreamed that a woman was standing over him in a field that went on forever. He swung around to her side, lost consciousness, and collapsed. The woman became his mother again. "I cannot utter a word because I am so tired," he wrote. "Comforted by my mother, I continue to sleep. Then I am already at my plot, digging with a hoe. Then she vanishes from the scene. I wonder if I can simply dismiss it as a dream?"

August 3 was devoted to digging the ditch. August 4 was again for farming. "Swoosh, swoosh. I heard the sound of a weed-cutting sickle." He vowed to make efficient work a lifelong goal. On August 5 he read from a book glorifying the *kamikaze,* in particular a smart young man of above average height named Lieutenant Colonel Seki. "He was always the top student throughout his school life. He took his responsibilities very seriously. It would take someone like that to become so distinguished to successfully crash his own aircraft into his target."

Among themselves, the boys talked about their families, each wondering when he would next be allowed to visit home.

On August 5, the teacher called in Fumio and two other boys. He announced that the next day they would be allowed to travel to Hiroshima. Fumio and the other two students were so excited they couldn't sleep. At three o'clock in the morning, their teacher confronted them for talking to one another. He ordered them to the emperor's shrine in the middle of the schoolyard to apologize for their lack of discipline. Each of them stood in the cold night air before the photographs and said they had made the mistake of staying up and talking, and they were sorry, and they would never do it again. The teacher then ordered them to apologize a second time. Fumio went back into the night and said, "Emperor and Empress, I'm sorry for what we said. We made noise." The teacher sent them back to the yard a third time. Again they repeated their humble apologies. By then it was four a.m.

The teacher said they need not pack for Hiroshima, because he was giving their passes to three other boys. Fumio was in tears at this lost opportunity to see his parents, as were his two classmates. He was later to determine that the three substitute boys arrived at Hiroshima Station at 8:05 a.m. on August 6.

Other than having had less than two hours of sleep, Fumio began the day with his fellows as usual. The students bowed to the emperor at the shrine and recited the Imperial Rescript on War. Fumio was one of about twenty students who were organized to go up the mountainside and continue excavating the water system. En route they saw two huge airplanes flying toward Hiroshima. There was no teacher in their work group, so they stopped to watch the airplanes. One of the airplanes rolled off sharply to the right and disappeared. One flew on, straight for the heart of their city. As they watched, it dropped a parachute, which some of the boys thought might be food but was actually a device to measure the impact of a blast. A single bomb plummeted to earth.

In the many accounts that followed, witnesses reported seeing and hearing widely divergent things. Fumio saw a yellow flash that was the most dense and vibrant color he ever had seen or imagined. He heard nothing. His teacher came along and told the boys that Hiroshima had been hit by napalm, which even then was one of America's favorite bombs. A fighting spirit rose within Fumio. "Hiroshima will stand firm," he wrote. "*Gambare!* (Be strong)."

He again prayed for the safety of his parents. He also wrote them a letter that he hoped would be delivered quickly. For his parents' sake, he vowed to do his best at all times.

Shortly thereafter, the boys went back to excavating the water system. In his diary, Fumio wrote, "We instinctively shouted that we could shoot them down if we had a fighter. The anger within us filled the silence."

The teacher repeated his belief that Hiroshima had been bombed by napalm. Fumio repeated his vow to do his best at all times. "Who is afraid of air raids?" he asked. "Just dig in and work!"

The next day a few survivors from Hiroshima straggled into the school area, wearing rags. Some wore only underwear. Their bodies were blackened and burned. One person's skin was falling off. Some were nearly blind. Fumio remembered them saying that when they ran outside of their dwellings, they saw the city had been leveled. A black rain had fallen on them from the sky but the fires nonetheless sprang up and began to feed off one another.

The next day, Fumio conceded that he arose feeling depressed. The school's definition of the American attack took a new twist. The boys were told the city had been destroyed by a powerful ray.

Uncharacteristically, Fumio swore: "Damn! I could not control myself. I hate the enemy!"

The next day, August 8, was the day of the month dedicated to paying especially prayerful respect to the emperor, and to pray for the nation to emerge victorious from the war. Fumio was bolstered. His first sentence was, "We will win the war!" He rededicated himself. "It was a clear, crisp day," he wrote, "perfect for work." He professed love for shoveling the sand off the cliff, a thousand grains at a time. The sand built up just the way his belief in winning the war built up. "To win the *Daitōa Sensō* (Greater East Asian War), we the students must work with all our might." He said if the students kept to their tasks, Hiroshima could be quickly rebuilt. "We must be firm in our belief in victory, serve our parents and teachers, destroy the most despicable United States and Great Britain, and relieve the Emperor of any worries."

The following day, August 9, Fumio was again beset by anxiety for his family. This was the day that the United States, unbeknown to the boys, dropped an atomic bomb on the southern city of Nagasaki.

Things were going from bad to worse. On August 9, Fumio was among a group of students who heard over the radio that the Union of Soviet Socialist Republics (USSR) had joined the war against Japan. He heard the announcement several times. "Each time I heard this message, I became very much frustrated," he wrote. "Come what may, we will beat the Russians!"

He was buoyed up by physical labor. On this day it was denied him because his teacher, Mr. Kodama, had gone into Hiroshima three days previously, and now he was ill. He was also ill on the following day, a Saturday. On Sunday, Mr. Kodama was reported, with great excitement, to be performing his work. However, his head always ached after going to Hiroshima. He also complained of fatigue. He listed four sets of the boys' parents as known to be safe, but the Miwas were not on his list. Fumio decided that their house in Yokogawa most likely had been demolished. "As I continued to listen to the teacher, I gnashed my teeth in helpless frustration," he wrote. "The question now is how we should proceed independently." The teacher suggested coping with the existing situation while finding a way to take revenge on behalf of their families.

August 13: Fumio, along with the rest of the boys, filed an application to go home. The teacher responded by giving them ten days off. Fumio tried to prepare himself to take care of his parents if they were alive or arrange a funeral if they were dead. He wrote, "I told myself I should remain calm in either case."

Interior pages of the diary reflect discipline and meticulous penmanship. (Miwa Family Collection)

August 14: "Keep working! Today is the last day of work before we leave for Hiroshima." Fumio watered the plants. He sprinkled night soil on the eggplants and the burdock. He attempted to cut weeds but was brought to a near halt by a thicket of bamboo.

August 15 was a Wednesday, the ninth day after the United States had dropped the Hiroshima bomb, which was becoming known to the world by the good-natured name of Little Boy.

Despite everything, the train was running, and Fumio found a seat. Arriving at Hiroshima Station, he was shocked that he could see in all directions. There were no buildings or trees to impede his view. He could even see the harbor. He wondered, "Is this the city we used to live in?" He felt empty as never before. For an incalculably long while, he stood staring. His only memory of this time was of standing, staring, and experiencing the shattering emptiness.

In his recollection, he wandered slowly from Hiroshima Station toward Yokogawa, passing by the now-empty site that for well over three hundred years had been the scene of Hiroshima Castle.

Charred lumber was everywhere. A quarter of a million homes had been destroyed.

At the Miwa house site in Yokogawa, only a half-burned pine tree was left standing, along with a fragment of the double fence. Everything else was flattened or had disappeared altogether.

Fumio sat another long while doing nothing. Likely night came and went while he wandered in this state of numbness and shock. He remembered the sky being perfectly blue. The day was hot. It was summertime. He felt devoid of any motivation. He thought everyone had died. He asked himself, "How could you escape from this?"

He set out for his school. He crossed the Ota River on the T-shaped Aioi Bridge. This was to become famous as the target of the bomb drop, although the actual hit would later be determined to have been several hundred meters away. He then passed the skeleton of the dome of the Industry and Commerce Building, previously a proud symbol of Hiroshima, and then wandered along the river to the site of his school. Its buildings had been built substantially of brick and concrete, and on the site he found some of its remains. He sat down in his schoolyard. Everywhere there was silence.

His mind was completely empty. He found a single tomato plant left curiously intact in the new garden he had seen on his prior visit. A single black tomato dangled from this one plant. He craved food and reached out to pick it, but something told him not to do so.

He retraced his walk, heading for his house site. Of the many hundreds of people who had died in the neighborhood, he saw only one blackened body. The others had been removed and cremated with astonishing speed. At first, he was not certain the person was dead, but he thought it probably was. The body was being eaten by maggots. He concluded that the person belatedly had crawled out of the rubble, only to die by the road. Fumio said a prayer for the person.

He sat around, staring for another long while at the wreckage of his home. The site had a water well. On the concrete wall of the well he found a written message. "Parents safe," it said, in his father's hand, along with an address of where his family could be found. Fumio was stunned that they had survived the vast ruin. He sat down again. He felt totally helpless. He felt as if he were floating through space, unable to gain traction with anything.

He could only think about food. He thought there was a point in the onset of hunger when a person can think of little else. Of his hunger he would subsequently write, "A moment of emptiness. You can't do worse than poverty and no food. What helped me was everybody else was starving."

He recognized an elderly couple from the neighborhood. They were building a shelter from scraps of lumber. "Having no particular schedule," with a newfound freedom from the regimentation of school, he stopped to help the two old people. He remembered a small bento box in his backpack, which he shared with them. As he left, they apologized to him for not being able to properly thank him. "Their words could not have made me happier," he later wrote. "I am so glad to be a part of their struggle to survive, though it was short."

At Yokogawa Station, he showed the conductor the address his father had left behind. He said he had no money. The conductor replied, "You know, kid, no one has any money. You're welcome."

He sat down with three adults on the train. He remembered that he had a handful of beans from the school in his pocket. He started eating. The three people looked at him, so he said, "Would you like to have a few beans?" All shared in his beans.

Disembarking, he walked long hours until at last he found the address. There is a cloud over whether all this happened in one day. In his memory it was a one-day event, but the distances involved, as well as his diary, suggest that it required a second day as well.

He returned to his diary on August 17. Most of his writing was about Japan's surrender to the United States, which had occurred simultaneously with his journey to Hiroshima. In the blur of events surrounding August 15 and 16, he recalled hearing the emperor's surrender statement either while he was on the train or as he arrived at Hiroshima Station. Addressing the Japanese public for the first time, the emperor said in his surprisingly high-pitched voice that circumstances compelled him to suspend the war against the United States, Great Britain, China, and the USSR. Despite the stilted language, Fumio grasped that Japan had lost the war. "Damn!" he wrote in his diary. "Tears of frustration began flowing down my cheeks."[1]

According to the broadcast's announcer, the emperor had ended hostilities "painfully aware" that new weapons could annihilate the entire population of Japan.[2]

"Ah," Fumio wrote, "how considerate His Imperial Majesty is to worry about us citizens! I was overwhelmed with emotion by his merciful concern."

The announcer reported that the Allied Powers had decided that Japan would be limited in size to its four main islands. Its far-flung empire henceforth would cease to exist. "Is this acceptable?" Fumio asked. "No, it is not. I feel so sorry for Amaterasu Omikami," a reference to the sun goddess.

He asked himself what he and his fellow students should do. "Isn't this the time for us to sacrifice our life for our country?" he wrote. "Winning or losing is a matter of luck.

"We have no choice but to give in at this time, but I (have) vowed to put all my efforts into the rebuilding of our nation."

CHAPTER EIGHT

The Explosion of Home

In the moment the bomb exploded, Seigo Miwa was inside a part of the house that had reinforced steel in the walls. Yoshio and Katherine were in a nearby warehouse of similarly solid construction. In the moments following the blast, the steel-reinforced part of the Miwa house stood for a crucial number of seconds, as did the steel-reinforced warehouse. For how long would later be a matter of speculation, but the results were indisputably measurable in human life. The superior construction of the two buildings kept them upright long enough for the Miwas to escape. This was the first crucial step of survival.

In contrast, many homes became death traps. They collapsed instantly and burned quickly. If people inside were not killed by the blast, they were trapped in what amounted to a pile of kindling. Stoves and cooking fires, thrown about, ignited the wood, and many people burned to death.

An old man named Shinsuke Uchiyama who lived a block away made three drawings of the neighborhood that were preserved in the archives of Hiroshima. Uchiyama filled his drawings with icons and notes. "Being an old man," he wrote, "I had a hard time drawing this map." On a second drawing he wrote, "There may be incorrect locations because of my vague memory." While apologizing for imperfections, he was determined to preserve on paper what was in his mind: "I cannot forget what I saw on that day."

Mr. Uchiyama had worked in the insurance section of the post office at the end of Miwa Street between 1923 and 1926. By the time of the blast, he was seventy-six years old.

His notes recalled what had existed before the bomb, together with what had happened that day. "People could hardly walk," he wrote, as fallen electric poles, wires, trees, etc. blocked the road." Just around the corner from Miwa Street, Uchiyama recorded: "Slippery road surface due to blood."

Across from the Miwas, Uchiyama indicated row houses of the Miwa tenants with the caption "Death toll, few hundred." He said at least one or two people had died in each house, indicating that many people had died on the spot, while more had gathered along Miwa Street and died of their wounds.

On the northern end of Fumio's childhood domain was a second note about multiple deaths: "Few hundred injured people lay on the floor [on a sheet of newspaper]." This note was associated with the savings and loan building across from the rail line. It showed stacks of bodies. Hundreds of people had taken shelter in a building fragment, creating the type of situation in which people lay side by side without medical treatment, dying in great numbers. Occasionally, with Herculean effort, the living would remove and stack the dead.

Countless people, suffering massive burns, threw themselves into whatever water they could get to. "Dozens of human remains floating on the stream," Uchiyama wrote. Across the Ota River, by the Yokogawa bridge, three short blocks from the Miwa compound, Uchiyama drew red flames raging from the roof of a Hongwanji Buddhist temple. "Few hundred persons who came to visit this temple died in the building," Uchiyama wrote.

By Uchiyama's count, about a thousand people had died in an area of several blocks between the rail line and the river. They had passed without any word other than Mr. Uchiyama's notes. To only one person, although nameless, he gave a story: "Body of the man who ran over my mother. He died of burns." Whether the man had run over his mother in the chaos of the bombing, or whether this had happened some time prior, Uchiyama did not say. The least penetrable of his three drawings was devoted to August 7, the day after the bombing. It depicted Miwa Street and an adjacent street. They were covered with big flecks, indicating fire. "This was the situation at 9:00 a.m., August 7," a note said. "The whole area was still engulfed in flame."

Where Fumio would say that when he looked across Hiroshima he saw nothing, Shinsuke Uchiyama saw in his mind's eye the thriving Yokogawa that had existed on the morning of August 6: a shrine called the Misasa Shrine, the elementary school, a needle factory, a rubber factory, dozens of stores, the row houses, the free-standing houses, and the Yokogawa town hall.

He made note of the Kamikawa family, whom he described as

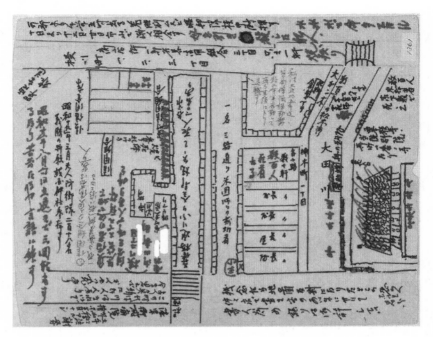

The Miwa neighborhood in the Yokogawa district of Hiroshima, as drawn by a survivor. (Courtesy of Hiroshima Peace Memorial Museum)

former residents of the United States. In two drawings he identified the "House of Senkichi Miwa (former resident of U.S.A.) (Owns many rental houses.)" Seigo had been master of the house since 1937, but in much of that time he had kept a low profile or been away in the U.S.A., and for seventy-six-year-old Mr. Uchiyama, young Seigo must have seemed almost transient—Seigo was never mentioned.

The bomb had been detonated across the Ota River from the Miwa house, between the domed Building of Industry and Fumio's school. The first kilometer outward came to be called the hypocenter. Previously the word *hypocenter* had referred to the point below Earth's surface from which earthquakes had erupted in all directions. The atomic bomb was a terrible quake that went downward. The Miwa house was in the next ring out from the hypocenter.

Katherine would remember emerging from a curtain of haze. "Are you all right?" her mother asked. They were covered with dirt. The building was shaking, and most buildings were already down. They climbed through a small window of the warehouse. At one house that

The devastation of Hiroshima, looking toward the iconic surviving Dome, was as Lawrence Miwa saw it on his return to Hiroshima after August 6, 1945. (U.S. National Archives)

was still standing, she saw people running in to get things, and then the house collapsed. As she looked at one man, his skin fell from his back.

Paper money was lying around. Some people paused to pick it up. Yoshio and Katherine ignored the money and set off running. They had a route in mind with a predetermined rendezvous point, thanks to Seigo, so they avoided the milling around that would be so deadly for so many people.

All their possessions were going down in ruin, and up in flames—the two swords of the samurai Marujiro, Seigo's phonograph, the library, and their multiple pianos. In the street, Seigo heard the shrieks of a woman emanating from a burning house. He tried to save her but the house was engulfed by fire. He too started running.

IN THE TWO PRECEDING YEARS, SEIGO Miwa had not only been playing cards and listening to music. By his awareness that Japan would lose the war, he was tremendously advantaged. On certain days he had gone to the countryside, about twenty minutes by train to the west. There he found a small two-story house belonging to his brother-in-law. Fumio would refer to it as a shack. It had a yard, and it was close to a river. Seigo made an agreement to rent the house and land, and he began planting vegetables. As a result of his foresight, he, his wife, and Katherine had an agreed-upon point of rendezvous, a shelter away from the city, and the beginnings of a garden.

Some days after the bomb, Seigo returned to Miwa Street and left the note for Fumio outside what had been their grand house. After his circuitous journey, Fumio knocked on the door of the address left to him by his father. He was exhausted and unsure of what to expect—unsure, even, that he had arrived at the right address. His mother answered the knock. They were miraculously reunited and filled with joy.

Seigo Miwa had never wanted the war. As a businessman, he needed peaceful conditions for his purpose of importing and exporting. After his return to Japan, he had not bought into the war psychology. He had endured it while watching out for his family's safety as best he could. As he had told his FBI interrogators over and over in Honolulu, he merely wanted peace between Japan and America.

Fumio, on the other hand, had lived all of his remembered life in the blare of military propaganda. Along with the rest of the country, Fumio had been conditioned to believe that Japan was invincible. The idea that Japan had not really been defeated held sway with him and many others for understandable reasons. Defeat on the battlefield had been limited to a certain number of Pacific islands that the United States had targeted, invaded, and then converted into bases for conducting the massive bombing raids against Japan's homeland. The Asian empire of Japan—Taiwan, Korea, Manchuria, northern China, the Philippines, and most of Southeast Asia—remained intact. Japan's enormous land armies in these areas were undefeated.[1]

Fumio was one among tens of millions who struggled to come to terms with the war's outcome. Had the horror and suffering been for naught?

By his reckoning, virtually all of his five thousand classmates from elementary school were dead. The third boy who had taken the test for middle school—the boy who had not been accepted—was dead. The three boys who had been awarded his pass from the school camp had arrived in Hiroshima Station about ten minutes before the explosion of the bomb. They were dead. One of his first cousins was dead, and the neighbors of his childhood were dead.

The destruction and chaos were such as to make counts of the dead and injured impossible. Hiroshima had been a city of more than a quarter million people. By one estimate more than a fourth of the population died instantly. Tens of thousands died thereafter of burns, other injuries, and radiation sickness.

The esteemed historian John Dower estimated that 2,700,000 Japanese died as a result of the war. Millions more were ill or wounded. Nearly a third of its people were made homeless. Most of the country's manufacturing capacity was destroyed.[2] The writer Kazuo Kawai recorded people beating battlefield helmets into pots and pans and carving wood scraps into clog sandals. Clothing was made out of pulp that, like paper, fell apart in the rain. "The extent to which the nation had been bled white in the war," Kawai wrote, "was almost beyond description."[3] Horrible, aching hunger was rampant, and starvation was not uncommon. Desperate people, who were often returning soldiers, roamed the countryside, stealing fruits and vegetables from farmers' fields. People ate grasshoppers, rats, and snakes, and added sawdust to their soup in an attempt to fill their stomachs.[4]

Since the moment of Commodore Perry's incursion and the beginning of the Meiji era, Japan had strategized, struggled, and fought to become, and to be recognized as, a first-class nation, free and sovereign, an equal to the imperialistic nations of the West. Now, in the public discussion, Japan had plunged from *ittō koku*, first rate, to *yontō koku*, fourth rate.[5]

How Fumio Miwa would bear up in these circumstances, and write about it in his diary, is one of the distinguishing aspects of his story.

In a ritual of continuity, Fumio's mother took him to the gravesite of his ancestors on his second day at the new house. They rose at 1 a.m. to buy a train ticket, securing a seat on a mid-morning train. They met some of his mother's relatives. Together they walked for three hours into the mountains. The graveyard was perfectly quiet. "I instinctively bow my head," Fumio wrote, "when I think about my ancestors and the likelihood that even now they are watching over us." The next day Fumio and his mother went back to Hiroshima and picked through the ashes of their house site. They found nothing.

On reading the text of the emperor's broadcast in a newspaper, Fumio experienced a renewed sense of outrage. His acceptance of the nation's surrender was hampered by the ambiguities of the emperor, who intoned, "The war situation has developed not necessarily to Japan's advantage, while the general trends of the world have all turned against her interest."

When Japan's military signed the surrender document aboard the U.S.S. *Missouri* in Tokyo Bay, Fumio wrote in his notes that he was infuriated. But he also wrote, "Now that the signing is over, I must forget the past and do my part to build a new nation."

As with most of the country, Fumio exempted the emperor from blame for the war. On the contrary, he wrote, "I praise him for his *samurai* spirit and for [his] expression of apology for not being able to reverse the unfavorable circumstances." To this he added a resounding prophecy: "Within a score of years or so, Japan will again be a great nation."

THE MYSTERY OF RADIATION SICKNESS WRACKED the family. Katherine was the sickest at first. Yoshio fed her castor oil and two raw eggs, which she retched up. Eventually Katherine would believe the raw eggs saved her life. Nonetheless she was so ill that she was put in a nearby hospital for several weeks. Yoshio also became badly ill and gave herself the raw egg treatment. She stayed in the hospital nursing Katherine.

Fumio stayed behind in the shack with his father. At the end of August, he was stricken with an attack of diarrhea so debilitating that he could hardly stand. His head spun. He was on a nearly all-vegetable diet, and Yoshio told him he had eaten too many vegetables, obscuring the likelihood that his own exposure to radiation had affected him. He was dead tired. When struggling with a mathematics lesson, he referred to yet another symptom of radiation. "How forgetful I've become," he wrote.

As time passed, it became painfully obvious that his mother's condition was the most dire of all. She was a small woman to begin with, weighing less than a hundred pounds. She lost ten pounds, and then another ten, another and yet another. She was disappearing. With her weight approaching fifty pounds, her condition miraculously stabilized, and she began a long, slow recovery.

IN THE EARLY DAYS OF SURRENDER, there was no functioning monetary system and no functioning local government. Rumors flew that Americans were on their way to attack, rape, and pillage the Japanese people. The journalist Kawai, an observer of the early occupation, described the Japanese as typically lethargic and apathetic. Kawai believed they were suffering from profound shock, as well as from a dietary intake that was around one-fifth of that of the average American soldier. "The defeat and the collapse of their old familiar world left them numb and dazed and deprived of any sense of direction or purpose."[6]

One of the nation's treasured sayings was, "Seven times down, eight times up," but in the aftermath of surrender the "up" was little in evidence. Analysts of the early occupation seized on the Japanese word for the psychological breakdown of an individual, *kyodatsu,* and used it to describe the condition of Japan's people as a whole.[7]

In extreme contrast, Seigo Miwa undertook a purposeful plan of action. He came to the fore of Fumio's existence, creating a role model of determined optimism. He had stashed away valuable artifacts, including Katherine's large collection of expensive *kimono,* which he sold off as a stopgap means of getting cash. He sold the pricey tea sets used in *chanoyu* and the intricate, stepped chests of drawers (*tansu*).

He acquired a large bag of salt, which was then a scarcity item. He traded part of it to farmers for a large bag of rice, as well as butter and jelly. Fumio would remember walking two hours to pick up a rice bag, then staggering home for four or five hours, at one point collapsing under its weight. His mother said he was the family's savior.

Central to Seigo Miwa's survival plan was a garden by the river. When Yoshio was away caring for Katherine, Seigo took Fumio to work in a plot filled with eggplant, cucumber, sweet potato, sesame, pumpkin, soybean, carrot, burdock, and sugar cane. Seigo and Fumio spread buckets of their feces in a newly tilled area and planted radishes. Seigo praised Fumio for all he had learned about plants during the evacuation. They dripped with sweat, working until dark.

They harvested their sugar cane. After cutting all the cane down,

Seigo said it was probably good for a gallon of molasses. Fumio was hoping for more.

Plants that grew underground became especially important. Round onions grew fast. Fumio would remember having onion soup for breakfast, fried onions for lunch, and boiled onions for dinner. This went on for months. He learned how to cook onions. One day he overdid the salt. His father laughed it off. "Men tend to think of cooking as something to be taken lightly, but that is not right," Fumio wrote. "Men should cook once in a while to understand how women feel."

The river—a tributary of the Ota River—tempted Fumio to rediscover swimming, even though he thought of himself as a weak swimmer. He stood on the riverbank, performing warm-up exercises and shouting encouragement to himself. He jumped into water that was twice as deep as he was tall. "I can swim!" he wrote. "The joy I felt was indescribable." At night after their labors, he and his father bathed in the river.

Father and son often went walking. One evening they struck out onto a mountain trail. They saw Japanese mushrooms growing and a farmer weeding his rice fields. They paused to study the farmer's technique. When they reached the mountain's peak, they saw their little house far in the distance. "Suddenly I felt invigorated," Fumio wrote, "like the flowing water in the stream—strange and wondrous indeed."

He had no books. "One could forget about reading," he wrote, "but being human one cannot give it up so easily." On one of their walks his father took him to a man named Mr. Imanaka, a *sensei,* who loaned him five books. "I went home a happy boy," Fumio wrote. "It has been a long time since I felt so eager and alive." He wanted to start reading right away but there was a power outage. "Someone said, 'A student should always have a book with him.' A gem of a saying, I thought." On their next trip to Mr. Imanaka, he borrowed Tolstoy's "What Men Live By." It was the story of a poor man who rescues a fallen angel, and eventually renders the key line, "I have now understood that though it seems to men that they live by care for themselves, in truth it is love alone by which they live. He who has love, is in God, and God is in him, for God is love."

Fumio thought Tolstoy's story a masterpiece. "[It] expands our understanding of truth in our ordinary lives." Reading, he became lost in time. "The morning hours passed like a dream. How happy I am! What a great time I had!"

Freed from the incessant directives of his school about what to think, he now thought about all manner of things. He wrote more expressively. Despite everything he had witnessed, he was excited about being alive.

Studying the night sky, he rediscovered the beauty of the moon. He said the moon had never fueled his emotions as it had on the night of August 28, 1945. "Mr. Moon," he wrote, "please light our way to the future." He said his prayers and renewed his oath to help rebuild Japan.

He described himself as struggling emotionally since his return to Hiroshima, and he again experienced a surge of anger. "Damn the enemies! The words suddenly spilled out." Several times his father went traveling. On one of these days Fumio had to wait at the train station for two hours for Seigo to return from Tokyo. This upset him. Previously Japan had been a world marvel for trains that ran exactly on time, and now the trains ran hours late.

His mother came home after twelve days of caring for Katherine. She praised him for his work in her absence. With Katherine still in the hospital and Shozo away in the army, he for once had both of his parents to himself. He gave thanks they were still alive.

On taking leave from school, Fumio had been told to return after fifteen days. It was a deadline that he took seriously, as if imagining the school's camp in the mountains still functioned. It was as he began making plans to depart on the first day of September that he fell ill, along with his parents. He began to suspect some sort of poisonous gas associated with the bomb. He nonetheless chastised himself. "Getting sick puts a burden on everyone," he wrote, "and I need to take preventive steps before it happens again."

Abruptly, on September 2, he decided not to return to the school camp. "My heart was not in it," he wrote. Whether there was a school to return to, he did not seem to know. Although now a self-directed student, he continued to make entries in his diary. He pressed forward with mathematics lessons and the study of Chinese characters.

FUMIO NOW FOUND HIS FATHER TO be as communicative as he had been before the war. In the face of tragedy, Seigo projected an aura of confidence. Possibly it was Seigo's broader view, encompassing an understanding not only of Japan but of Hawai'i and the United States, that saved the family from the deep agony of defeat.

Fumio overheard his father tell his mother that their properties in Hawai'i had been confiscated, and that his investments in the Japanese stock market were now gone. Seigo seemed to be unfazed, and his mother took the news of financial disaster philosophically. Under their influence, Fumio's patriotic anger was increasingly transformed into an affirmation of daily life. From this he formulated one of his bedrock beliefs: "If you've lost everything and you're at the bottom, you're going to expect to gain a little bit. Life is too short to be pessimistic."

The first occupation forces that Fumio witnessed were Australians, a localized rarity in the flood of occupying American troops. When the Australian troops moved into an area called Kurugahama Beach north of Hiroshima, Seigo quickly struck up a relationship with them. After the Australians had built their camp, they had lumber left over. He told them he would be glad to get the lumber out of their way, to which they agreed. He then gave the lumber to a group of Japanese carpenters on the condition that they use part of it to build him a new house, which they did. The family moved out of their shack into a comfortable three-bedroom house on a lot overlooking the ocean.

When Seigo had written from Lordsburg to Ambassador Joseph Grew, seeking work as a translator with the American forces, the untimeliness of his letter had caused it to be lost in the shuffle. Nonetheless the thought remained, and Seigo now landed a job translating for the American occupation force.

Although his businesses were in shambles, the family now had income and a good house. Seigo's symptoms of radiation poisoning were brief, as were Fumio's. Katherine was recovering. Yoshio was slowly getting better as well. Shozo returned from army service in the autumn of 1945. He had been stationed on the Pacific Ocean side of Shikoku Island, across from Hiroshima. He was one of the many inexperienced soldiers who had been deployed to fight to the death in defense of the homeland. Weirdly, the atomic bomb probably had contributed to his survival.

The combined effects of environmental devastation and radiation sickness made the family's return to Hiroshima unworkable. One day, Seigo came home and abruptly announced they were being moved by American soldiers to Kure City, where Seigo continued to work for the American army.

Fumio remembered moving into yet another comfortable house. About a third of the Kure City's housing still stood. Kure City had a thriving black market, which was conducted from rows of blankets on the ground or off tabletops in the open air. Fumio bought his first eyeglasses from a street vendor, who gave him an eye test as they stood on the sidewalk. The glasses worked.

After three months of independent study, Fumio returned

to middle school. To get to the school ground, he first had to walk through a blackened tunnel, feeling his way by hand, frightened by the unknown. On the other side he met a school bus, which was propelled by a wood-burning fire. When the bus came to a hill, it stalled, and he and the other riders got out and pushed.

As part of the new education policy formulated by the occupation, the schools had been ordered to eliminate the teaching of "ethics" (which often had served as the code word for military indoctrination), geography (which in the moment of surrender had reduced Japan from far-flung empire to its four home islands), history, martial arts, and the military training of students.[8] As a result, Fumio suddenly experienced a new type of schooling. If vaguely, he was migrating from a system of received learning to reflection, and from intensely prescribed behavior to a more exploratory system.[9]

Having been encompassed from infancy by Japan in its most militarized years, he had thought of the oppressive controls of the imperial state as merely how life was. As learning became more open-ended, he acquired a new slant on the United States. He specifically credited an English language class that was taught by a Japanese man who was fluent in English. In the exercises, Fumio learned about democracy. Intellectually, this was the start of a conscious realization that he had been subjected to brainwashing. The high tide of his fervent notions about Japan and the emperor receded.

Seigo Miwa helped this process along. He confided to Katherine that he regretted his return to Japan and wished that he had stayed in the United States, so that now he would be back in the Territory of Hawai'i. He began to tell stories of how he had migrated to the islands as a teenager, and how he had acquired an education, and how America then had given him a chance to succeed in business. Fumio was taken with this image, in no small part because he realized his father could well have harbored a deep bitterness towards America. The American government, after all, had denied Seigo a path of naturalization to citizenship, despite his being a third-generation resident. It had confiscated his property. It had interned him in the southern New Mexico desert. Finally, it had A-bombed him and his family.

Fumio began to think of the United States not as the enemy but as a land of opportunity, and Hawai'i became, in his mind, a shimmering paradise. He was fifteen. "I'm a kid," he thought. "I'll take a chance." Brother Shozo, although likewise born in Hawai'i, was not a part of this conversation because, the Miwas believed, his service in the Japanese

Fumio Lawrence Miwa's Kure Middle School class photo, 1946. He is in the third row, second from the right. (Miwa Family Collection)

army barred him from returning to America—this despite the fact that Shozo had no choice but to serve Japan.

Under the guidance of Seigo Miwa, Fumio and Katherine boarded a slow train to Tokyo. Japanese soldiers—returning home by the thousands—barged through the train doors and crawled through the windows, abandoning their former discipline. As Fumio traveled north, he could see that not only Hiroshima but the entire Pacific-facing industrial complex of Japan was largely destroyed.

After a ten-hour trip, they arrived at a strangely quiet Tokyo. There were only a few cars in the streets. They did not have directions to the American embassy but didn't need them. From the train station, they saw two sizable buildings standing out from the ruins of the great city. One was the Imperial Palace, and one was the American embassy.

Fumio did not grasp that, as a matter of birth, he was an American. Because all of his memories were of Japan, and his entire sense of citizenship and nationality was of Japan, it never occurred to him until late in life, as he reviewed things, that his American citizenship was inherent in his birth on American soil and unbroken across time. At the embassy he thought of himself as getting American citizenship "back," which he and Katherine did with seeming ease. They returned to Kure City with American passports and with assigned berths on a converted troop carrier.

They said goodbye to their mother at home. Fumio reassured her that all would be well. Seigo accompanied them to Kobe Harbor, where Katherine broke down and wept. Fumio felt himself tearing up, but his father was upbeat. "I will see you in Hawai'i," he said. By the time Fumio and Katherine boarded and found a place on the railing of the ship, they could see their father walking away in the distance. "Dad," Fumio said to himself, "why don't you turn and look at us once more?"

The ship was called the S.S. *Gordon,* famous in its time for its contribution to unscrambling the vast dislocations of humanity in the war. It sailed with only a few Japanese. Most of the passengers were Filipinos who had boarded in Manila or Chinese who had boarded in Hong Kong. Males bunked on one side of the ship and females on the other, so that in the seven days at sea, Fumio and Katherine seldom saw one another. People generally did not converse. There was a strange absence of shipboard socializing.

Fumio was intensely curious. He walked the deck, studying the passengers and the ocean. People lined up to eat in a mess hall style, and Fumio ate all the variety and volume of food he wanted for the first

Fumio Lawrence and Katherine Miwa came to Hawai'i on the same passport, issued by the United States embassy in Tokyo, June, 1947. (Miwa Family Collection)

time in years. En route, he turned sixteen. To celebrate his birthday, he asked Katherine for change to buy a soda. Katherine was twenty-four. She carried their money, which amounted to less than fifty dollars. She said no, then turned away, weeping for his disappointment. In terms of cash on hand, they were as poor as the low-ranking *samurai* Marujiro had been when he had first traveled to the Kingdom of Hawai'i to work in the sugarcane fields.

The *Gordon* passed the island of Kaua'i and swung along the south side of O'ahu, passing Pearl Harbor. It continued along the leeward side of the island beneath the dramatic peaks of the Wai'anae and Ko'olau mountains into Honolulu Harbor, docking on July 9, 1947. Fumio had an American nickel. In his excitement, he threw it overboard to the Hawaiian boys who dove for coins in the harbor.

PART IV

Home

CHAPTER NINE

Tadaima in America

From the moment of his arrival, Fumio became known by his American name, Lawrence F. Miwa, or Larry Miwa. He and Katherine were met by the general manager of the Miwa Store. This was not to suggest that things would be taken care of for them. The manager and his wife lived in a house that previously had belonged to the Miwas. Larry was told that he and Katherine could live in one room, provided that he start working in the warehouse immediately. Larry began lugging rice bags and preparing produce for sale.

It did not take him long to realize that the Miwa properties were out of his family's control. The manager was aloof, and government officials were showing an uncommon interest in the store.

Larry well could have been disheartened, but he was not. On the contrary, his bad memories of the war were giving way to imagining a bright future. He worked systematically at forgetting Hiroshima and the atomic bomb. He concentrated on looking ahead. He was bursting to learn everything he could about the United States. His attitude was, "Go forward, and see what I can do."

New acquaintances told him he should go to school. The logical choice was his father's alma mater, Mills School, by now known as Mid-Pacific Institute. In the missionary tradition of Hawai'i, Mid-Pacific Institute maintained a particular concern for immigrants. Larry was accepted as a full-time boarding student in the fall semester of 1947. He was one of two boys from Japan. A third immigrant was from Korea. In a class picture of seventy-eight students, the largest number were of local Japanese ancestry, with a sprinkling of Chinese, haole, and Filipino. The class was coeducational but boys predominated.

The thumbnail caption in the student annual was about Larry blending in: "His wide friendly smile sends a glow of warmth to everyone." The annual described him as a first-class mathematician. Also, he often could be found on the tennis court. At first, he was a member of the junior varsity; in his senior year he was on the varsity. During 1951, he was a member of the International Club, reflecting the school's Pacific-oriented tradition and its participation in the Institute of Pacific Relations. The club presided over a series of interschool meetings devoted to the study of China, which had turned Communist two years previously. The club also studied Japan, which was still under U.S. occupation; Korea, which was teetering on the edge of civil war; and India, which through nonviolent resistance had just wrested its independence from its colonizer, Britain. International Club members discussed events within these countries as well as the U.S. foreign policy toward each.

What the school annual could not convey were the extraordinary circumstances of Larry's existence at Mid-Pacific Institute. Tuition was five hundred dollars a semester, an astronomical figure for a student with no financial support. The school administration told him his tuition would be waived if he worked. He served food in the dining room and washed dishes in the school kitchen. He mowed the lawn of the boys' school. He also mowed outside the girls' dormitory, but only after struggling with self-consciousness, having spent virtually all his life with boys.

During the school year, cafeteria food was free and abundant. He was never hungry. In the three months of summer vacation, he worked in the carpentry shop. He slept in the dormitory, alone. He survived on Campbell's soup, which he heated on a Bunsen burner in the chemistry lab. At one point he broke an arm. He got free treatment and quickly returned to work. He started growing again, and sprouted from under five feet to five feet two inches.

During his first year, he struggled with learning English, but thereafter his proficiency picked up momentum. He had come to Hawai'i with his English-class notions of democracy. Now he studied constitutions, the rule of law, and elections, all of which strengthened his favorable impressions of democratic government. He felt he had been constantly watched in Japan, but now he was impressed that people spoke freely about a wide range of subjects, personally as well as publicly. He realized that life in Japan was organized around obedience to the emperor. Now he felt unbound. To his great surprise, he found himself changing his mind about Japan and the United States. He asked, "What makes America great? What made Japan lose?"

He thought it was in his nature to be outgoing and friendly, to engage with people, and to explore ideas. He thought this was his real self and that it was coming to the fore in Hawai'i.

Narrow obedience was no longer a paramount virtue. He began to think in terms of emulation. He came to regard his father as a practitioner of independence and self-direction. Where discipline had been imposed in Japan, his new discipline was self-imposed. With no one to tell him what to do, he told himself what to do. He interpreted the culture of Japan as saying, "You have to do your best for the interest of the national government." He interpreted American culture as saying, "You have to do your best for yourself." Although he was making earth-shaking changes in his ideas about life, he was still driven by the potent words of his mother. In his sleep he heard her say, "Do your best."

He trained himself to get by on four hours' sleep, a habit he would maintain for decades. In addition to his workload, he played tennis as much as two hours a day.

Meanwhile, Katherine moved into a house that she shared with four other young women. She began working as a waitress. She married a Japanese American man, and she continued waiting tables. On weekends she would pick up Larry and take him to her house, where he did his laundry.

Before Larry departed from Japan, his father had talked with him about trying to regain ownership of the family's property in Hawai'i. For a fifteen-year-old who spoke little English, it was too big of a notion. By 1949, many aliens from Axis nations were regaining their U.S. assets, but not the Miwas or, generally, people who had lived in their "country of origin" during the war.

The U.S. government had taken control of the Miwas' stores and associated houses, and Larry and Katherine watched as their potential wealth was broken into pieces and auctioned off.

Despite the auction, Seigo Miwa was not about to give up. If he was not to regain control, he was determined to get restitution for a wrongful taking, and his agent for doing so had become Larry.

Meanwhile, Larry worked his way through Mid-Pacific Institute in four years. He applied to several colleges and was accepted by both the University of Hawai'i and the University of Denver. Denver offered him a one-year scholarship, and Larry accepted, with the idea of broadening his base of experience and learning about the North American continent. Possibly it was no accident that the offer had come from Colorado. When the federal government had forced the evacuation of the Japanese community from the coastal states, Colorado's governor

Fumio Lawrence Miwa mastered English, mastered coursework, and supported himself through a progression of schools and universities, accumulating academic honors along the way. (Miwa Family Collection)

uniquely had struck a welcoming note, and Colorado generally had a reputation for treating Japanese more fairly than did the other Western states.

The grit that Larry had shown at Mid-Pacific Institute was similarly evident in Denver. He moved into a boardinghouse near Japan Town. The landlord gave him the option of living rent-free if he agreed to take care of elderly boarders. He was sent to the basement, where he found decrepit old people living in filth, their clothes and bedding soiled. Larry washed them, changed their clothes, and changed their bedding.

Thereafter he moved into a private home closer to the university. He shared a room and got a job as an assistant houseboy. When snow fell, he shoveled pathways through the snow before dawn. He vacuumed, did the laundry, folded clothes, and washed dishes. He was usually finished with his household duties around 7:30 p.m. and turned to his studies. Eventually he got a job in the school library, working from 1 to 9 p.m. and then studying far into the night. He came to believe he could take notes in class and sleep at the same time.

In an economics class, he struck up an acquaintance with the professor, a man named Byron L. Johnson. Johnson would talk for forty minutes about economics and then for twenty minutes about current events and world history. He held the unusual view that people of Japanese ancestry had gotten a raw deal at the hands of the U.S. government during the war. He was interested in Larry's story, and particularly in the fact that the Miwa properties had been taken over and auctioned away.

Larry thought of himself and Professor Johnson as free birds who were unfettered by conventional thought. Johnson was a flaming idealist. Like Johnson, Larry was hot to pursue his goals and to right wrongs. He worked even harder in school.

He felt his father's presence, which worked on him as a call to action. He recalled Seigo's idea of retrieving the family properties. He began to think that perhaps justice could be done after all because the United States prided itself on living by the rule of law.

Meanwhile, Seigo wrote Larry a letter saying that he had been experiencing stomach problems, and that he had undergone surgery. Ever the optimist, Seigo believed that he was recovering. He was confident that in a few months he would be well.

Shortly thereafter Larry received a second letter, this one from his mother. It said that his father had not been told that he had cancer—a widespread practice at the time, even more so in Japan than in the United States. He had only a short while to live.

Seigo again wrote to Larry saying that he still hoped for the family's sake to be compensated for his assets. Between Katherine and Larry, Larry was now the logical option. He could read, write, and speak English fluently and was rapidly gaining an education in American business practice.

Larry tried desperately to raise money to visit his father. He wrote to a prominent Japanese American journalist in Denver who happened to be Seigo's cousin, promising to repay a loan for travel money. The journalist replied that he didn't have that kind of money.

Seigo continued to hope that he could return to Hawai'i. It remained the place of his dreams. He died on May 23, 1954, at the age of fifty-seven. His ashes were placed in the family graveyard in Furuichi with his ancestors.

When Larry received the death notice in a letter from his mother, he lost control and wept effusively. He was to think of his father's death as the lowest point in his life, notwithstanding all else he had been through. He blamed his father's early demise on radiation poisoning. Larry still had his mother, who seemed to have recovered, but he now felt he was alone in carrying forward his family responsibilities. In Larry's mind, achieving restitution became more than an issue of fairness.

He saw it as honoring his father and clearing the family's name. He hoped, in the process, to validate what he regarded as the best of American traditions: fair play and democracy.

Researching his father's transactions, Larry realized Seigo had returned to Hawai'i in October 1941 because he was worried about losing his properties in the event of war. Seigo had engaged two of Honolulu's foremost attorneys, Robert Murakami and Masaji Marumoto. He had converted his businesses from his sole ownership to a Hawai'i corporation. He had given his manager a small fraction of his stocks—apparently in an attempt to engage him in a more binding relationship. He then had signed operational control of the business over to his manager through a power-of-attorney declaration. However, neither the incorporation nor the power of attorney had proven to be an adequate shield. Following his return to Japan in 1944, his properties had been confiscated by the Alien Property Custodian of the U.S. government.

The Alien Property Custodian was an obscure and hurriedly conceived agency of the war. Its basis in law would be criticized by Supreme Court Justice Felix Frankfurter as "a makeshift patchwork." While its expressed purpose was to hold the assets of interned aliens for the duration, the more shadowed side of the operation was its liquidation of such assets.

Hoping to regain what he thought of as rightfully his, Seigo Miwa asked to return to Hawai'i in 1947. His request was denied by the U.S. government on the grounds that, first, he had willingly left the United States and, second, that he had then resided in an enemy country.

When the twenty-four-year-old Katherine and sixteen-year-old Larry thereafter returned to Hawai'i, Seigo had written a will naming Katherine—as an adult American citizen—the sole heir to his properties in Hawai'i. He then filed a claim with the U.S. Office of Alien Property, attempting to recoup his stores in Hawai'i, as well as his bonds and bank accounts, and to transfer ownership to Katherine.

In this filing he argued what proved to be the two recurring points of both his residency case and his property case. His first point was that he had left the United States under duress. His second was that on his arrival in Japan, he had played no part in Japan's war effort and, on the contrary, had lived in a state of oppression at the hands of Japan's government.

In his correspondence, Seigo cited a conversation with an immigration officer in El Paso, Texas, that occurred before he was shipped cross-country to the *Gripsholm*. Seigo said he was asked whether he really wanted to be repatriated to Japan. He reported replying that he was motivated not by patriotic affinity to Japan but by the fact that his mother was dying: "[I] was informed by a letter through the neutral channel that my aged mother was hopelessly ill, and she wanted me to be at her bedside." The neutral channel in question would have been the communication channel through Switzerland and Spain. His mother had died while he was en route to Hiroshima.

At the 1949 auction of the Miwa assets, the Alien Property Office sold his stock in J. S. Miwa Ltd., including ownership of the Kalihi and Mōʻiliʻili stores, for $130,000. His household furnishings were auctioned for $49. The government continued to hold $4,000 in accounts payable to the San Francisco import business, as well as U.S. savings bonds of $100 and $50; cash in Liberty Bank in Honolulu in the amount of $520.46; the five bonds issued by the prewar government of Japan with a face value of $1,000 each; and a certificate of deposit to the government of Japan with a face value of 37,799 yen. In the estimate of the U.S. government, this rounded out to an "account," as it was called, of just under $150,000. In correspondence, Seigo valued his assets at $1,000,000, and Larry would later argue for a value of $290,000.

The remaining asset under government control was a life insurance policy with a face value of $4,075. As a young man, Seigo had taken out the policy, naming the infant Katherine as beneficiary. Each spring, he recorded in perfect script in a small notebook paying the insurance company a premium of $204.75. The U.S. government liquidated Katherine's policy and pocketed the cash.

In 1952, Yoshio wrote to U.S. President Harry S. Truman and the then ambassador to Japan, Robert D. Murphy, reasserting Seigo's claim. The acting chief for claims in the Alien Property Office responded to her letter by saying that he would either recommend allowing the claim or set up a formal hearing before an examiner. Two years passed without a further word or hearing.

One of Seigo's last acts was to write another will—the will naming Larry as his sole heir. As with his previous will, his goal continued to be finding a strategy for securing his one-time American assets for his family.

While in Denver in 1954, Larry began to work on the alien property case in earnest. He contacted an attorney named Minoru Yasui, who eventually would become known throughout the country as one of four persons of Japanese ancestry who had resisted the forced evacuation through the U.S. court system during the war. At the time of

Larry's contact, Yasui was a struggling lawyer in Denver's Japan Town, sometimes accepting payment for his services in chickens or fruits and vegetables.[1] Yasui advised Larry that he was fighting an uphill battle but he nonetheless took the case. Robert Murakami also continued to follow the case in Hawai'i, so young Larry quickly had the services of two of the most distinguished Japanese American attorneys in the country.

By this time, America had abruptly ended the occupation of Japan and employed Japan as a base for projection of U.S. military force against the spread of Communism in Asia. Japan rapidly was becoming less a defeated dependent and more of an ally.

In the national media of the United States, occasional articles began to appear describing Japanese Americans as model citizens. Indeed, the emerging description of Japanese American virtue was often their alleged inclination to suffer injustice and discrimination in silence. The internment of aliens such as Seigo, followed by the wholesale roundup of Japanese American citizens, was at this point not publicly questioned. The internment was in fact so little discussed that it was known only to the victims and to a relatively few conscience-stricken individuals such as Professor Johnson. Despite the scattered stirrings of a change in public opinion, both in regard to Japan and to Japanese Americans, the climate for the Miwa alien property case continued to be chilly.

Meanwhile, the longer Larry lived in Denver, the more he became aware of subtle and not so subtle forms of racial discrimination. His stint as a houseboy, for example, was straight out of the Hollywood stereotyping of Asians. He was eager to move on. He raced through the University of Denver's four-year program in three years, graduating with an A-minus average. For his effort, he was invited to join the Phi Beta Kappa honor society. He knew virtually nothing about it and was not inclined to attend the induction ceremony. A university administrator took him aside and told him that excellent food would be served, at which point Larry acquiesced. Classmates dressed him in wear that was formal if oversized. The majority of those honored were women, which caused him to ponder the likelihood that women were equal in intelligence to men, and possibly more so.

Thinking of New York as a more cosmopolitan and open city than Denver, he applied to the graduate school of business at the prestigious New York University. He was admitted and, again, was given a scholarship to help support his first year.

Professor Johnson, soon to be a successful candidate for the Colorado State Legislature, suggested that en route he stop over in

Washington, D.C., and confer with an attorney friend of his named Oliver E. Stone. Larry set out to cross the eastern half of the American continent in late August. Where he had once had a nickel in his pocket on arrival in Hawai'i, he now had one hundred and fifty dollars. He took a Greyhound bus through Kansas and Missouri and on east to the nation's capital.

He found Stone to be an idealist in the spirit of Professor Johnson. Stone previously had served as an attorney for Congress's Intergovernmental Committee on Refugees. Like Johnson, he thought people of Japanese ancestry in America had been singled out during the war for grossly unfair treatment.

Stone took the Miwa case on a contingency of ten percent of whatever settlement might ensue. The ten percent figure was the maximum allowed under the law. If this ceiling was intended to protect aliens from exploitation by lawyers, it was nonetheless a low figure in the world of contingencies, and it was a particularly low figure for fighting such a difficult legal battle. As such, it likely discouraged many lawyers and many potential plaintiffs from pursuing alien claims. Nonetheless, with no hourly billing and the maximum one-tenth contingency, Stone tore into the case with gusto.

LARRY STAYED WITH A FRIEND OF Professor Johnson's for five nights in Washington, D.C., while he and Stone talked their way through his case. He then went on to New York. Arriving in the great city late at night, he went to the downtown YMCA but was told he should have made a reservation two months in advance. On 34th Street he saw a neon sign advertising a room for five dollars a night. The real price was fifteen dollars, which he split with a friend. He stayed one night but could not sleep because of the street noise. The next day he found a room for seven dollars a week that he shared with another friend. Larry slept on the floor and his friend slept on the bed. They used a communal bath down the hall.

Surrounded by a sea of whites and blacks, Larry thought of himself as one of only a few Asians in the city. After an initial surge of excitement, he was sobered by the intensity and impersonality of life in New York. Everything seemed to move faster than Denver and immeasurably faster than Honolulu. Larry thought one would either sink or swim in New York, and in the first few weeks he feared he might sink. He returned to the daily pattern that had carried him through Mid-Pacific Institute and the University of Denver. He went to classes in the morning, then worked an eight-hour day in a print shop. He studied late into the night, barely slept, and started over the next day.

While juggling his studies, he began working long distance with his brother Shozo, who was trying to penetrate the U.S. market with whatever Japanese exports seemed the most promising. As Shozo's representative, Larry set out to import Japanese textiles. This was an uphill proposition, because the stamp "Made in Japan" in the early postwar years was still synonymous with items being poorly made.

He formed a relationship with an import/export businessman named Bernard Preyer, who was interested in Larry's ideas and also interested in the reviving economy of Japan. Preyer gave Larry a job, then introduced him to a buyer for the retailing giant J. C. Penney, Inc. In pursuit of a sale, Larry made a study of the textile business. In addition to his university studies, he enrolled at Preyer's suggestion in the trend-setting Fashion Institute of Technology, where he became conversant in such things as design, thread counts, tensile strength, and quality control.

On the finance side, he immersed himself in issues of product licensing, market positioning, and critical-path production. He worked out agreements between Japan and the United States via tedious exchanges of letters, which he translated himself on weekends. Because of the high cost of international telephone calls, this was his only medium of communication.

In mid-1957, his hard work began to pay off. J. C. Penney placed an order through him with Preyer for twelve thousand baby overalls. The order was plagued by a lack of operating capital. At one point, buyer and seller even disagreed over who would pay for the design and fabrication of the prototype. Worse, Shozo's suppliers in Japan were not in line to be paid for several months. At a point when Larry had fifty dollars to his name, he set out to raise $36,000 in bridge financing. He got to know a Japanese banker who worked with Sumitomo Bank's New York agency in Manhattan. The banker guided Larry through various real-world lessons in finance, then announced that with $6,000 up front from Preyer, Larry could secure the $36,000 credit. Everyone agreed, and the transaction worked to the advantage of all concerned.

Despite his successes, Larry felt the New York business culture was often based on manipulation and sometimes on outright deception. In response, he vowed to be straightforward and never to manipulate or dissemble. Treating everyone courteously and fairly, he concluded, was the most important thing he could do. It was good business. It also was a reflection of his positive frame of mind, which had evoked such positive responses from people like the attorney Stone and Professor Johnson.

While Larry thought of himself as trusting by nature, in New York he began thinking more consciously about whom he could trust. He cultivated the art of making quick studies of people he met, relying on a balance of intuition and analysis that, he believed, allowed him to predict a person's character with great accuracy.

IN TWO YEARS HE COMPLETED A master's degree in business administration with an emphasis on accounting, graduating with a B+ average. In addition to his membership in Phi Beta Kappa, he was made a member of the international business fraternity Beta Gamma Sigma.

Preyer then sent him to Japan, instructing him to look around quietly for good investments. Larry perceived the reviving Japan as a contradiction. "I was indeed surprised to find many elaborate coffee shops, movie theaters, and new modern department stores in the cities I visited," he wrote to his mentor Johnson. "But behind those buildings, most of the people [are] struggling for a day-to-day living."

After eleven years away, he reunited with his family. He was now twenty-seven years old. His mother announced that he should consider getting married. She said she was off to meet the Binjiro Kudo family, previously of Honolulu, and suggested that Larry go with her. This was the same Kudo who, prior to the war, had been acting consul general in Honolulu, and who once had been Seigo's golfing partner. The Kudos had five daughters.

The fourth daughter, Yoko, was a graduate of Sacred Heart College near Takarazuka, outside the city of Osaka. Where Yoko was eventually to speak of the Miwas' bad luck, possibly she thought of hers as particularly good. After leaving Honolulu, her father had been reassigned to Canton, the dominant southern city of China. When the war ended, he and his family were stuck in hostile territory. Staggering numbers of Japanese shared this plight—upwards of two million in China, and well over one million in Manchuria, for example.[2] Throughout Japan's erstwhile empire, Japanese were hunted down, harassed, and sometimes killed. The Kudos, after running and hiding, were spirited to safety on a Japanese ship. Binjiro Kudo regrouped by opening a law practice in Osaka, and by the time of Larry's visit in 1958 he was doing well. Larry and Yoko began dating. The families employed the traditional middlemen to intercede. Gifts were exchanged, Larry quickly proposed, and Yoko accepted.

Larry and Yoko Miwa married in Japan, then settled in America, December 10, 1958. (Miwa Family Collection)

Larry and his bride Yoko relax at a friend's New York City apartment, April 1960. (Miwa Family Collection)

They were married in a Catholic church out of deference to the Kudo family's religion, which in the postwar period had become more acceptable in Japan. Although Seigo Miwa had been a baptized Christian, Larry considered himself a Buddhist, but generally for him religion was not an issue. After the wedding, he left for New York to find a better apartment and buy furniture, and then Yoko joined him.

From Larry's first contact with Stone in the summer of 1954 to January 1959, Stone actively pursued the Miwa claims case in Washington, D.C. When he informed Larry that the case was not going well, Larry wrote back, "From purely the ethical and democratic standpoint, I sincerely believe that what belonged to our family once should be returned to me. I wish that humanity and not the results of legal torment will prevail on us, if America still upholds the sense of integrity for her people."

With Larry's active assists, Stone won skirmishes. For example, a government claims officer erroneously asserted that Seigo had spent the entire war in Japan when, quite obviously, he had not—he had lived in Honolulu and then been interned at length in New Mexico. Government agents also contended that Seigo had spent a majority of his life in Japan, when in fact he had lived more of his life in Hawai'i. In yet another instance, the government contended that Seigo did not have a house in Hawai'i, when in fact he had owned a string of houses, the last of which seemed to have disappeared in the government's confiscation of his property. Seigo's last will, making Larry his sole heir and successor-in-interest, was at issue, but was eventually validated. Also, the small stock share assigned to Seigo's manager in Hawai'i created confusion but was sorted out, albeit to no real effect.

In all, these errors reflected a pattern of the U.S. government making suppositions that were untrue—in the interest of marginalizing Seigo Miwa's status. U.S. officials clung to two contentions: first, that Seigo had not departed from the United States under duress but rather of his own free will; and, second, that he had been a resident and citizen of legal standing in the enemy state of Japan.

The question of whether Seigo Miwa had left the United States under duress was the simpler of the two issues, although less than straightforward. "Viewing his life as a whole," Stone wrote, "one must conclude that Seigo Miwa's activities and sympathies center more in Hawai'i than anywhere else." This was likely even more true than Stone could imagine, since Seigo was, if not an American citizen, a third-generation immigrant to Hawai'i. "His main holdings and business interests always remained at his main office which was in Hawai'i. Although he languished for a year and a half being shunted around in various American internment camps, and was then returned to Japan while under deportation order, as soon as the war was over he repeatedly sought to return to his home in Hawai'i."

Hawai'i, Stone argued, "remained his place of residence as long as he had freedom of choice in the matter. Had he not been uprooted and interned and returned to Japan by the United States Government authorities, no question could arise in this case as to whether his presence in Japan constituted residence. As it happened, he lacked control over the events."[3]

The U.S. government continued to maintain that when Seigo

had left in the prisoner exchange, he had repatriated—that is, he had returned to Japan to resume his Japanese citizenship. As to Stone's contention that Seigo had lived in a state of oppression in Japan, the Claims Section chief demanded proof of "some law, decree or regulation of the Japanese Government directed against political, racial, or religious groups."

Stone cited a statement of the U.S. Immigration and Naturalization Service acknowledging that when Miwa had left the country in the prisoner exchange, he had been under an order of deportation. He argued that Miwa could not have been both involuntarily deported and voluntarily repatriated. It was one or the other.

The second issue, of his having lived in a state of oppression in Japan, was more complicated. Early on, Larry wrote that such evidence likely was "destroyed by the atomic bomb dropped on our house in Hiroshima." From Hawai'i, the attorney Murakami advised against pursuing this avenue, since he believed the impetus for this provision of the law was to allow claims by Jews, Poles, gypsies, and others in Europe who had been persecuted by Germany.

Stone advised to the contrary. In line with Stone's guidance, Larry addressed the case with a renewed passion on receipt of a narrative written by his mother, which he translated for Stone. "His [Seigo's] life in Japan was very miserable during the last war," she began. "He had been always watched by military police. When he was in Hiroshima, he firmly rejected Mr. Uchida, the military policeman, who had asked about the domestic conditions of the United States.

"He refused to work for the Intelligence Bureau which offered him a high salary," she went on. "Because of his refusal, he was constantly followed by policemen, even when going out for a short walk." To support this description of Seigo's life in Yokogawa, she appended a sworn statement from a neighbor, a man named Toshiko Kawano, who wrote, "I know the fact that [Seigo Miwa] was very often questioned of his daily conduct by the national policemen who, therefore, oppressed his freedom."

Yoshio portrayed the family finances of wartime as his children would recall many years later: that is, Seigo had no job and no business. He and the family lived off rental income. This contention was supported by a man named Manabu Terada, former executive director of the Marusan Rubber Company, who swore that as of March 1941, Seigo was "retired" from his role as company director and thereafter "was not concerned at all with the affairs of said company."

Yoshio recalled that as American bombing spread across Japan, the city government of Hiroshima had condemned five of the Miwa rentals, which were torn down and removed to create a fire break in the event of a firestorm. "This shows," Yoshio wrote, "the apparent persecution against him by the then city government of Hiroshima."

She portrayed him as having been isolated by his adoption of Christianity at Mid-Pacific Institute: "He was christened while in Hawai'i and could not religiously link himself with the rest of the Japanese people in the community."

Seigo Miwa had been approached to not only participate in the neighborhood organization (*tonarigumi*), but to be the head of it. "Again he firmly refused," Yoshio wrote. For this he was "regarded as disloyal against the war-time government by some." The neighbor Kawano provided a supporting statement saying that Seigo "was denounced and ousted as a man who had never attended the meetings of '*Tonarigumi*,' and who refused to become the head of the said organization when requested."

Yoshio portrayed Seigo's postwar relationship with the American army as a response to a request from the police commissioner who previously had harassed him. "As soon as the war ended," she wrote, "Japan was put in [a] state of utmost confusion by various rumors in regard to the American troops on her land. She needed good contactmen between her people and American soldiers." The police commissioner recalled Miwa's American ties and "begged him to carry out the smooth landing of American troops at Hiroshima as well as Kure City."

At the time, two aspects of the repatriation issue were ignored for lack of information that would only begin to emerge much later. These had to do with the shrouded events of the civilian prisoner exchange. The first was the fact that Japan had so much leverage that it effectively chose the people it wished to repatriate. Second, in America's eagerness to satisfy Japan, certain U.S. residents of Japanese ancestry, even Japanese Americans, were shipped to Japan without their consent.

On April 8, 1958, the hearing examiner issued his finding. He wrote that even if it was true that Seigo Miwa was interrogated and spied upon, and even if it was true that Miwa was criticized for not participating in the neighborhood *tonarigumi*, Stone's briefs nonetheless had failed to make a case for reversing the government's position. "No specific Japanese laws, decrees or regulations are cited," the examiner wrote, "nor is there any evidence of any such substantial deprivation of citizenship rights by reason of official action."

In effect, the U.S. government's ruling ignored the fact that Japan's military regime enforced a level of conformity that was beyond the realm of law, decree, or regulation. By extension, the ruling ignored the U.S. conception of Japan between 1941 and 1945 as an authoritarian state. Neither the filing nor the response discussed the fact that wartime Japan was a closed society, under the constant surveillance of the secret police.

Accordingly, the truth of Miwa's circumstances in Japan was obscured by a cloak of purposeful amnesia. In the rapidly changing international climate of the Cold War, Japan's brutal dictatorship was something Japan *wished* to forget and that America *needed* to ignore in context of its newfound enthusiasm for Japan as the shield against the rapid spread of Asian communism.

Nonetheless, Stone and Larry were not through fighting. They appealed the hearing officer's decision to the United States Attorney General, William P. Rogers.[4] Although much of their written appeal was a rehashing, Stone sharpened it, bearing down on the contention that Seigo Miwa, through no fault of his own, had left the United States under a deportation order and therefore, by definition, had been under duress. They waited. Larry fretted over whether the appeal was being heard. Stone wrote back assuring him that it was—Stone, in fact, had face-to-face contact with high-level figures in the Justice Department. After yet another round of filings, in early January 1959 the Attorney General rejected their appeal.

Larry read the rejection letter in his tiny, dormitory-like room in upper Manhattan. This was where—for him—the curtain fell. He realized the case was never going to succeed. The idea of clearing the family name and retrieving a fraction of the family's wealth was effectively over. In memory, his reading of the letter was a grievous experience second only to the death of his father and his wandering through the A-bombed Hiroshima. "There is something striking my heart," he wrote to Stone, "that is, I would not know really what to say to my father, if he was alive today."[5] Larry thanked Stone kindly for his efforts. He acknowledged that the case had been enormously difficult and said that the U.S. laws in question were harsh.

Having neither the luxury of time nor the inclination to mope, Larry picked himself up yet again. He and Yoko resolved to put the rejection out of their minds and move forward. Within a few weeks, Larry barely thought about it.

COINCIDENT WITH COMPLETING HIS MASTER'S DEGREE in business, the climate for people of Japanese ancestry in the United States was changing. Shortly after his 1959 return from Japan, Larry was hired first by one small investment house, Arnott Baker and Co., and then by a second, McDonnell and Company. At McDonnell, he passed the test to qualify as a security account executive and worked as a broker and adviser for securities and investing.

He was no longer a bone-thin immigrant student with a big smile but, rather, was an educated, bilingual Japanese American with a position in a brokerage house. Japan's postwar status was being normalized and its culture admired. Its resurgence worked in his favor. Preyer visited Japan and announced that he hoped to stay for a year. Oliver Stone was so proud of a Japanese painting given to him by the Miwas that he hung it on the wall behind his desk. Larry later gave him a Japanese vase as well, which Stone displayed in his office anteroom. Stone wrote saying how pleased he was to make Yoko's acquaintance and asking Larry what stocks he should buy.

Crazily, an entire group of people who had been marginalized or imprisoned only a few years previously were now being held up as exemplary citizens. Economists were talking up a Japanese Miracle. In 1959, Hawai'i was admitted as the first majority Asian-ancestry state, significantly based on the record of its Japanese American war heroes. One third of Hawai'i's population was of Japanese ancestry, and the war-wounded and highly decorated Daniel K. Inouye was immediately elected to the U.S. House. The portrayal of Japanese Americans as the model minority was now being widely employed by newspapers and magazines.

In 1961, Larry and Yoko moved from New York to Los Angeles, where he became assistant manager of a new West Coast office of his securities company. There he gained firsthand experience in investment banking and initial public offerings. The company newsletter ran a long story about him as a Horatio Alger figure—that is, as a self-made man. The article breezed past the dense history of the Miwa migrations by saying that Larry had gone to Japan for education as a small child and returned to Hawai'i to attend high school. In an ahistorical country, in what way did such a complicated backstory matter?

Stephen Miwa was born in 1963, the first of four children. All were born in California. In a letter to Oliver Stone, Larry wrote that Stephen was good at both basketball and baseball. In 1973, Larry moved the family to Hawai'i, where he was employed in the international

Larry, left, with older brother Shozo and sister Katherine, in reconstructed Yokogawa, September 2, 1982. (Miwa Family Collection)

Larry and Yoko Miwa with their young family: (left to right) Stephen, James, Jacqueline, and Edward, late 1970s. (Miwa Family Collection)

division of the Bank of Hawai'i, a business of the old-line missionary interests. He then was hired into the international banking division of the most quintessentially Nisei of Hawai'i's business institutions, the Central Pacific Bank, which was founded by the veterans of the 100th Battalion/442nd Regimental Combat Team, known by their shorthand as the most decorated per man unit in the history of U.S. warfare.

On making the acquaintance of a second Japanese American congressman, Spark M. Matsunaga, Larry relived his alien property case. Matsunaga at first suggested special legislation. Time passed. Eventually Larry's case and others were consolidated into a single bill. This initiative morphed into a more broadly based movement for reparation and apology to all of the living victims of the forced evacuation and incarceration of 1942–1945. Famously, this bill passed in 1988 as the Civil Liberties Act. Each beneficiary received a signed letter of apology from the president of the United States and a check for $20,000. Larry and Katherine were ineligible by virtue of having spent the war in Japan.

Larry's mother, Yoshio, miraculously lived to be ninety-one years old, despite the severity of her radiation sickness. Larry's wife Yoko died in 1999 at the age of sixty-four. Larry retired from Central Pacific Bank before her death but could not sit still in retirement. A former colleague from CPB invited him to co-found a new bank, which they called the Pacific Rim Bank.[6] Far into his eighties, Larry continued to work full time, exuding optimism about the future and, overall, an authentic sense of joy. What was said of him as a school student could have been said of him in his eighties: "His wide friendly smile sends a glow of warmth to everyone."

The Hiroshima government designated August 19, 1945, as the cutoff date for persons who had entered the city after the bomb to be considered bomb survivors. Since Larry had entered on August 15, he became one of the last survivors so acknowledged.

Throughout his life, he occasionally suffered from a stomach upset that may or may not have been related to radiation poisoning. His overall energy level remained extraordinarily high, of the type one has if he or she is glad to be alive.

EPILOGUE

Over the course of our shared exploration of the past, Stephen Miwa changed subtly. At first he had been preoccupied with the case for retrieving the Miwa assets. He was disturbed by the injustice of it all, of which there was plenty to go around. The more he studied, the more his thoughts migrated back to Hiroshima. He stared into the inhumanities of the war between Japan and America. He began to think of our work together as a small contribution to the prayer that such a thing never happen again. In the process, he discovered something of himself as a Japanese American, with an obligation to contribute to his transnational legacy.

As to his mother's statement, "The Miwas are unlucky," he came to the opposite conclusion. The Miwas were lucky. He felt intently that he owed his existence to a long skein of good fortune: to Seigo Miwa's 1943 return to Japan and his organizing the family for survival; to Larry's admittance to his middle school, which resulted in his evacuation from the city of Hiroshima; to the headmaster's freakish punishment of Larry for whispering to his friends, which kept him from traveling to Hiroshima on the day of the atomic bomb; and, finally, even to the intuitive voice that told Larry in the schoolyard not to eat the burned tomato. Stephen's list went on.

One day, I told him about my own visit to the Hiroshima Peace Center. I recalled that as I looked at the immensely sad and terrifying exhibits, I shored up my emotional floodgates by telling myself something like, "This is not about you, Tom. You're here to learn and gather information. Keep moving." At the end of the exhibits, there is a shelf where visitors are invited to leave comments. Along with the hundreds of thousands of ordinary people who pass through the Center, the politically mighty or morally great figures from around the world leave their notes here. As I thought about whether I might attempt a drop-box

147

Stephen and Larry Miwa, 2017. (Photo by author)

comment, I mistakenly picked up several copies of the one-page form for doing so. By accident I dropped the forms on the floor. I picked up each one carefully. I obsessed over putting each form as neatly into a stack as possible. I tapped the edges, hoping that nothing would hang out irregularly. I was unable to write anything. As I told Stephen this story, my hands began to tremble.

Stephen organized his own expedition to Japan around the August 6, 2015, Seventieth Anniversary of the first atomic bombing of human beings. He returned to Miwa Street, to the original house site, to the site of his father's school, to the family graveyard in the mountains, and even to the house, still standing, which his grandfather Seigo had built from the Australian army's lumber during the Occupation.

On the day of the Seventieth Anniversary, he rose at 5 a.m., thinking he would beat the crowd. Despite the early hour, the streets were already swimming with people seeking to be involved in the remembrance. A Buddhist sect passed out floating paper lanterns, and Stephen carefully wrote the names of his known ancestors on them: Marujiro, Senkichi, Seigo, Larry, his mother, and finally himself, his wife Carrie, and his daughter Chloe. He also wrote my name. He stood in line a long while, moving forward five abreast, until finally he had space to release his lanterns into the Ota River. With the thousands, they slowly floated away to the sea.

NOTES

Chapter 1: A Samurai's Journey to Hawai'i

1. Mikiso Hane, *Modern Japan: A Historical Survey, 2nd ed.* (Oxford: Westview Press, 1992), 93–94.

2. Alan Takeo Moriyama, *Imingaisha: Japanese Emigration Companies and Hawaii, 1894–1908* (Honolulu: University of Hawai'i Press, 1985), 124–125.

3. *The Friend*, February 1895, 7.

Chapter 2: The Merchant's Story

1. James H. Okahata, *A History of Japanese in Hawai'i* (Honolulu: United Japanese Society of Hawai'i, 1971), 152.

Chapter 3: Turning a Profit

1. This conclusion is based on information found at Japan's National Museum of Immigration at Yokohama.

2. Translation of January 18, 1940, *Nippu Jiji* story on J. S. Miwa courtesy of Tatsumi Hayashi, volunteer, Japanese Cultural Center of Hawai'i.

3. Regarding the *Nippu Jiji* claim that Seigo Miwa was associated with the national cabinet of Japan: There is no supporting evidence for this idea.

4. The *Tatsuta Maru,* built for the NYK line in 1929, was originally named the *Tatuta Maru* (without the "s"). It was renamed in 1938. To avoid confusion, it is referred to throughout as the *Tatsuta Maru.*

5. Tom Coffman, *Nation Within: The History of the American Occupation of Hawai'i* (Durham, N.C.: Duke University Press, 2016), 213.

6. Only one more passenger ship was to arrive from Japan in Honolulu, the *Taiyo Maru.* It carried several spies who made last-moment checks on targets. The *Taiyo Maru* would be sunk by an American submarine in early 1942 in the seas south of Japan.

Chapter 4: Interned by the USA

1. James Seigo Miwa was also referred to in a few sources as Shogo Miwa.

2. Suikei Furuya, *An Internment Odyssey: Haisho Tenten* (Honolulu: Japanese Cultural Center of Hawai'i, 2017), 32.

3. Furuya, *An Internment Odyssey,* 14.

4. Kazuo Miyamoto, *Hawaii: The End of the Rainbow* (Tokyo: Charles E. Tuttle Company, Inc., 1964), 322.

5. Yasutaro Soga, *Life behind Barbed Wire: The World War II Internment Memoirs of a Hawai'i Issei* , trans. Kihei Hirai (Honolulu: University of Hawai'i Press, 2008), 48.

6. Soga, *Life behind Barbed Wire,* 60.

7. Patsy Sumie Saiki, *Ganbare! An Example of Japanese Spirit* (Honolulu: Mutual Publishing, 2004), 119.

8. Soga, *Life behind Barbed Wire*, 118.

9. Gail Honda, ed., *Family Torn Apart: The Internment Story of the Otokichi Muin Ozaki Family* (Honolulu: Japanese Cultural Center of Hawai'i, 2012), 66.

10. Saiki, *Ganbare!*, 121.

11. Soga, *Life behind Barbed Wire*, 79.

Chapter 5: Traded to Japan

1. Translation to English, along with publication, only recently has made a composite picture of Lordsburg possible. The accounts of Soga, Ozaki, and Furuya were developed through the determined work of the Japanese Cultural Center of Hawai'i. The Hoshida story was published by the Japanese American National Museum of Los Angeles.

2. Dennis M. Ogawa, foreword to Soga, *Life Behind Barbed Wire*, xii.

3. Soga, *Life behind Barbed Wire*, 25–26.

4. The Japanese language edition was published in 1948.

5. Soga, *Life behind Barbed Wire*, 105.

6. Soga, *Life behind Barbed Wire*, 107.

7. Soga, *Life behind Barbed Wire*, 89.

8. Honda, *Family Torn Apart*, 30.

9. Honda, *Family Torn Apart*, 30.

10. Honda, *Family Torn Apart*, 69.

11. Honda, *Family Torn Apart*, 90.

12. Honda, *Family Torn Apart*, 91.

13. Saiki, *Ganbare!*, 79, 145. Hoshida's wife subsequently was one of those who signed up to be reunited with her husband. She put their severely disabled daughter in Waimano Home and took the other three children to the camp in Jerome, Arkansas, where she waited for more than a year to be reunited with her husband.

14. P. Scott Corbett, *Quiet Passages: The Exchange of Civilians between the United States and Japan during the Second World War* (Kent, Ohio: The Kent State University Press, 1987), 2.

15. Corbett, *Quiet Passages*, 17.

16. Specifically, it conjured the 1920 London Naval Conference, which limited the Japanese navy to three-fifths the size of the U.S. and British navies; the defeat of Japan's resolution on human equality in the League of Nations; and, worst of all, the Japanese Exclusion Act of 1924.

17. Bruce Elleman, *Japanese-American Civilian Prisoner Exchanges and Detention Camps, 1941–45* (New York: Routledge, 2006); for a detailed explanation of how the negotiations evolved, see 12–14.

18. Max Hill, *Exchange Ship* (New York: Farrar & Rinehart, Inc., 1942), 6.

19. Hill, *Exchange Ship*, 198.

20. Furuya, *An Internment Odyssey*, 79. The writer was at Camp McCoy at the time.

21. Elleman, *Japanese-American Civilian Prisoner Exchanges*, 116.

22. Hill, *Exchange Ship*, 158.

23. Honda, *Family Torn Apart*, 57–58; also Furuya, *An Internment Odyssey*, 159.

24. Honda, *Family Torn Apart*, 57–58.

25. Corbett, *Quiet Passages*, 195.

26. Furuya, *An Internment Odyssey*, 190.

27. Corbett, *Quiet Passages*, 74.

28. See Corbett, *Quiet Passages*, on 74, 84, 86.

29. Furuya, *An Internment Odyssey*, 80. He also counted five Hawai'i men in the first exchange (see 95). He stayed in the United States as a result of pressure from his family (96), like Ozaki. "When I realized I had finally made the decision to stay permanently in America," Furuya wrote, "I was overwhelmed by a sense of loneliness" (119).

30. In Corbett's research, 737 of 1340, see *Quiet Passages*, 93.

31. Honda, *Family Torn Apart*, 63.

32. Tomi Kaizawa Knaefler, *Our House Divided: Seven Japanese American Families in World War II* (Honolulu: University of Hawai'i Press, 1993), 49. Based on a 1966 interview with his daughter Jane.

33. Knaefler, *Our House Divided*, 49.

34. Atsushi Archie Miyamoto, MSS, in Archives and Special Collections, University Library, California State University, Dominguez Hills (Carson, CA, 2008); see http://www.csudh.edu/archives/csudh/index.html. Miyamoto eventually became a lieutenant colonel in the United States Army.

Chapter 6: Coming of Age in Hiroshima

1. Raymond Lamont-Brown, *Kempeitai: Japan's Dreaded Military Police* (Gloucestershire: Sutton Publishing, 1998), vii, also 16.

2. Kazuo Kawai, *Japan's American Interlude* (1960; Chicago: University of Chicago Press, 1979), 44.

3. Kawai put Japanese conformity in the following context: "The nation's martial traditions, popular habits of docility in the face of authority, the emperor myth, and other such historic factors provided an environment which offered little natural immunity to the appeals of the militarist agitators" (*Japan's American Interlude*, 44).

4. The ratio of German soldiers taken prisoner against those killed was roughly fifty-fifty. Ulrich A. Straus, *The Anguish of Surrender: Japanese POWs of World War II* (Seattle: University of Washington Press, 2003), 39.

5. Strauss, *The Anguish of Surrender*, 49.

6. Strauss, *The Anguish of Surrender*, 29–34.

Chapter 7: A Schoolboy's Diary

1. Ian Buruma, *The Wages of Guilt: Memories of War in Germany and Japan* (New York: Farrar, Straus and Giroux, 1994), 80–81: "In virtually every group, someone—generally a woman—broke out in a gasping sob. Then the men, who with contorted features had been trying to stay their tears, also quickly broke down. Within a few minutes almost everyone was weeping unabashedly as a wave of emotion engulfed the populace." "There surged up in the people a deep

sorrow over the pain the Emperor must have endured in calling upon them to bear with him this national humiliation."

2. Buruma, *The Wages of Guilt,* 37. Buruma had a particularly pungent description of the Emperor's appeal in defeat: "Close to three million Japanese were dead, many more wounded or seriously ill, and the country in ruins as a consequence of the war waged in the emperor's name, yet it was his agony on which his loyal subjects were expected to dwell." Hirohito was to say that when he contemplated the suffering of Japan's people, "my vital organs are torn asunder."

Chapter 8: The Explosion of Home

1. See, for example, Ronald H. Spector, *In the Ruins of Empire: The Japanese Surrender and the Battle for Postwar Asia* (New York: Random House, 2007), for an understanding of Japan's military forces on the Asian continent, an accounting obscured by the narratives of the bomb, American victory, and the Occupation.

2. John W. Dower, *Embracing Defeat: Japan in the Wake of World War II* (New York: W. W. Norton, 1999), 45.

3. Kawai, *Japan's American Interlude,* 134.

4. Dower, *Embracing Defeat,* 91.

5. Dower, *Embracing Defeat,* 44.

6. Kawai, *Japan's American Interlude,* 139.

7. Dower, *Embracing Defeat,* 89.

8. Kawai, *Japan's American Interlude,* 187, also Dower, *Embracing Defeat,* 84.

9. Kawai, *Japan's American Interlude,* 73.

Chapter 9: *Tadaima* in America

1. Densho Encyclopedia online http://encyclopedia.densho.org/Minoru_Yasui/.

2. Dower, *Embracing Defeat,* 49.

3. In the matter of Lawrence Fumio Miwa, as Successor-in-interest to Seigo Miwa, Title Claim, 26 Nov. 1958, No. 36891, p. 6.

4. Rogers served briefly as Attorney General under President Eisenhower, whose term ended in 1960. He became better known as President Nixon's Secretary of State, starting in 1968.

5. Lawrence Miwa to Oliver Stone, 23 Jan. 1959.

6. Lawrence Miwa worked part time for City Bank, 2002–2006, before joining Pacific Rim Bank (later renamed First Foundation Bank) as a senior vice president and director.

In the text, I have limited endnotes to documenting crucial facts and crediting the unique work of other writers. In addition, I want to convey something I think readers are owed: a statement of sources that most influenced the act of writing.

The key family documents, which Stephen Miwa pried out and organized, created a genealogical spine, particularly the multigenerational *koseki,* or family record, derived from the village of Furuichi, Hiroshima Prefecture, Japan. As a result of the dialogue between Stephen and his father, Larry Miwa shared his student "self-reflection diary" spanning the months before and after the atomic bomb. Tatsumi Hayashi, a volunteer at the Japanese Cultural Center of Hawai'i, translated these and other documents into English, without which we could not have proceeded. Correspondence by Larry Miwa as he attempted to retrieve compensation for the family property in Hawai'i was preserved by him and organized into a large file by Stephen.

I interviewed Larry three times on videotape at length and, informally, several more times as the writing moved forward. I also videotaped a long interview with his sister Katherine.

In its exhibits on the prewar, the Hiroshima Peace Center provided an informative picture of how the settlement at Hiroshima evolved. The Hiroshima city archive shared the drawings of the Yokogawa neighborhood by Shinsuke Uchiyama. The Japanese *Who's Who* of prewar business in Hawai'i came from the prefectural archive. These and other finds resulted from the efforts of Dr. Kosuke Harayama of the Japanese National History Museum in Chiba City and his associate, Kaori Akiyama. Dr. Harayama and Ms. Akiyama were, and remain, committed to developing transnational U.S.–Japan history.

Tomi Kaizawa Knaefler's book, *Our House Divided: Seven Japanese American Families in World War II* (1991), originally published serially in 1966 by her newspaper, the *Honolulu Star-Bulletin,* was an early day revelation of families being divided between Japan and Hawai'i. Most recently, Pamela Rotner Sakamoto takes up the divided-family story of a renowned Japanese American soldier, Harry Fukuhara, in *Midnight in Broad Daylight: A Japanese American Family Caught between Two Worlds* (2017). Leslie Helm's *Yokohama Yankee: My Family's Five Generations as Outsiders in Japan* (2013) is good reading. In an academic vein, the Center for Japanese Studies at the University of Hawai'i enlarged on the definition of binational history via a 2001 conference that I was privileged to attend. Key participants included Dr. Noriko Shimada of Japan and Dr. Paul F. Hooper of Hawai'i. The work of the conference was published by the University of Hawai'i Press as *Hawai'i at the Crossroads of the U.S. and Japan before the Pacific War* (ed. Jon Thares Davidann, 2008). The existence of all such work encouraged me to think that transnational stories were accessible.

James Seigo Miwa's "hearing" with the martial law government panel is part of his record in the U.S. National Archive. His experience in the Justice Department's camp at Lordsburg, New Mexico, posed a challenge to add something meaningful to an already overflowing field of inquiry around internment. As one well-known Japanese American scholar once remarked to me, "The internment is becoming a cottage industry." The starting point for making greater sense of internment is the careful definition of an intergovernmental system developed in Dr. Tetsuden Kashima's *Judgment without Trial: Japanese American Imprisonment during World War II* (2003).

The description of Japanese militarism as manifested at the Lordsburg, New Mexico, internment camp rests mainly on three excellent works translated by the Japanese Cultural Center of Hawai'i. These are Yasutaro Soga's *Life behind Barbed Wire: The World War II Internment Memoirs of a Hawaii Issei* (2007), Otokichi Ozaki's *Family Torn Apart: The Internment Story of the Otokichi Muin Ozaki Family* (ed. Gail Honda, 2012), and Suikei Furuya's *An Internment Odyssey: Haisho Tenten* (2017). Additionally, the JCCH research program pointed me to two additional oral interviews on file in their rapidly expanding database.

For a step-by-step narrative of Japan's interior history, I relied on the survey *Modern Japan: A Historical Survey* (2nd ed., 1992) by Mikiso Hane. For binational exploration of the love/hate dynamics between the United States and Japan, I frequently have turned to Dr. Akira Iriye's *Power and Culture: The Japanese-American War, 1941–1945* (1981) and Dr. Walter LaFeber's *The Clash: U.S.–Japanese Relations throughout History* (1997).

Ship manifests, which tracked the international travel of the Miwa family, now can be conveniently retrieved through Ancestry.com. The changing nature of the forms over time, as well as the notations, are of historic importance. The question of travel eventually progressed from the prewar to Seigo Miwa's wartime participation in the U.S.–Japan civilian prisoner exchange. Other than the fact of top-level ambassadors and diplomats being swapped, the subject of prisoner exchanges has been slow to develop. I was introduced to the story of the second civilian exchange by interviewing Latin Americans of Japanese ancestry who had been shanghaied into the Crystal City, Texas, camp, several of whom were later shipped to war-torn Japan. These interviews resulted from the invitation of an internee friend, Kay Uno Kaneko, who included me in a camp reunion in 2008.

Among the few published sources, Bruce Elleman's 2006 *Japanese-American Civilian Prisoner Exchanges and Detention Camps, 1941–1945* unearthed important information but somewhat jumped the tracks, at least in my view, with his contention that the demands of prisoner exchange were behind the U.S. internment policy. *Quiet Passages: The Exchange of Civilians between the United States and Japan during the Second World War* (1987) by P. Scott Corbett is the best source I could find. Most recently *The Train to Crystal City: FDR's Secret Prisoner Exchange Program and America's Only Family Internment Camp during World War II* (2015) by Jan Jarboe Russell puts an anguished human face on the exchange.

As I saw how the last-minute sailing of passenger liners was negotiated between the contending countries, it altered for me the definition of when the war started. I came to think that we of the United States were engaged in a death dance with Japan prior to December 7. Accordingly, I believe the civilian prisoner exchange warrants further examination.

As for the postwar, Ronald H. Spector's *In the Ruins of Empire: The Japanese Surrender and the Battle for Postwar Asia* (2008) creates a much broader (that is, Asian) understanding of Japan's surrender than generally exists in the standard American view.

The effect of the occupation on Larry Miwa, as well as how the war is remembered, brought forth a heap of reading. Foremost, no surprise, was John W. Dower's weighty and monumental *Embracing Defeat: Japan in the Wake of World War II* (1999) followed by Ian Buruma's *The Wages of Guilt: Memories of War in Germany and Japan* (1994). Kazuo Kawai's *Japan's American Interlude* ([1960] 1979) is also a good source.

Readers of early drafts shared much-appreciated insights and critiques: Michi Kodama-Nishimoto, the long-time practitioner of oral history at the University of Hawai'i; the esteemed teacher and author Elinor Langer; Dr. Tetsuden Kashima, historian of the internment; Rena Arakawa, a Miwa family friend; and Brian Niiya, content director of the Densho website project and editor of the Densho Japanese America Encyclopedia.

A personal note seems appropriate to the exploratory writing of a transnational story. I settled in Hawai'i in 1965 at age twenty-two, when Japanese American influence in the new fiftieth state was peaking. Things Japanese in origin—Japanese slang, restaurants, bars, tea houses, temples, movies, television broadcasts, slippers, and eating ware—were ubiquitous. These were fascinating elements that floated in the multicultural mix of Hawai'i. When I actually traveled to Japan, the pieces gained order. I have been to Japan eight times on trips of a week to several weeks, usually to do with media production or writing work. Since a person could spend many years there and still be an outsider, obviously my experience is not a claim to expertise. Rather, it is an indication of longstanding interest and a desire to learn.

Finally, I am deeply grateful to Stephen Miwa for seeking me out and to Larry Miwa for opening himself without qualification to my questions. Also to Katherine Sato (née Miwa). Their verve and enthusiasm for living are an inspiration.

INDEX

Adoption, 3, 14
Akiyama, Kaori, x, 153
Alien Property, 132–134, 146
Amaterasu Omikami, 7, 92, 109
Angel Island, 55
Archives of Hawai'i, 4, 7
Archives, Hiroshima, xi, 110, 153
Archives, U.S. National, 47, 76–77,
    94, 113, 154
Atherton, Frank, 24, 35
Atomic bomb, August 6, 1945: dev-
    astation, 104, 110, 115; disori-
    entation, 143; hypocenter, 112;
    reconnaissance, 94; Seventieth
    Anniversary, 148; survivor of,
    146; U.S. experiment, 93

Banking: Bank of Hawai'i, 146; Cen-
    tral Pacific Bank, 146; Pacific Rim
    Bank, 146
Bicknell, George H., 52
Bicultural house (Miwa), 31–32, 91
Big Five: of Hawai'i elite, 15–16, 35,
    42; Japanese, 83
Bishop Museum, 28
Bombing: country-wide, 93, 115; fire
    breaks in Hiroshima, 94, 224. *See
    also* atomic bomb
Brazil, 68
Buruma, Ian, 151nn1–2; 155
Bushidō, 79, 92

China, 12–14, 35, 38, 46, 56, 137
Chūshingura, 62, 100
Citizenship laws, 14–15, 46, 71; bar-
    ring J. S. Miwa, 43; Katherine
    Miwa, 30; Lawrence F. Miwa, 30,
    83, 123. *See also* dual citizenship;
    Japanese Exclusion Act
Cole, Ralph, 35
Constitutional rights, 52

Corbett, P. Scott, 150nn14–15,
    151nn27–28, 155
Council for Interracial Unity, 36
Crystal City Internment Camp, 71–72,
    78, 155
Customs, U.S. forms, 10, 15, 38–39.
    See also ship manifests

Denver University, 129, 133–135
Diplomacy, Spain and Switzerland, 67,
    69–70, 73, 133
Dole, Sanford, 9
Dower, John, 115, 152n2, 155
Dual citizenship, 30, 48–53, 83, 123

Education: of J. S. Miwa, 24–25, 46;
    of Lawrence Fumio Miwa, 87–96,
    98, 100, 102–108, 118, 121,
    127–131
Elleman, Bruce, 150n17, 150n21, 155
Emmons, Delos C., 43, 73–74
Emperors: Hirohito, 98; Meiji, 152

Farrington, Joseph R., 35
FBI, 37, 39, 41–44, 78
Fort Sam Houston, 56
Forty-seven Ronin. *See* Chūshingura
Frankfurter, Felix, 132
Fukunaga Case, 84
Funeral/grave, 116, 148; Senkichi, 31;
    J. S. Miwa, 148
Furuichi (Village), 4–5, 8, 11, 13, 18
Furuya, Suikei, 61, 68, 74, 149nn2–4,
    150n1, 150n20, 151n23, 151n26,
    151n29, 154
Fuzoku Chugakko, 92

Gambare, 104
Geneva Convention, 55, 65
Gentleman's Agreement of 1907, 17
Goa, Port of, 78

Goto, Y. Baron, 42, 44
Green, Thomas H., 52
Grew, Joseph, 66, 68, 72–73, 120
Group that Supports the 100-Year War, 68

Hamilton, John, 35
Hane, Mikiso, 149n1, 154
Harayama, Kosuke, x–xi, 153
Hawai'i, Kingdom of, 6–7, 15
Hawai'i, Republic of, 10, 14–15, 40
Hawai'i, Territory of, 13–17, 33–35, 40–48, 84
Hawai'i Netsu, 7
Hay, Feed and Grain, 16, 18
Hayashi, Tatsumi, 149n2, 153
Helm, Leslie, 154
Hill, Max, 68, 70, 150nn18–19, 150n22
Hiroshima. *See* Atomic Bomb; Archives of Hiroshima
Hiroshima, Castle, 3–4, 12, 32, 107
Hiroshima, development of, 4–5
Hiroshima, Industry and Commerce Building, 92, 107
Hiroshima, Peace Center, 147, 153
Honda, Gail, 150n9
Honor Societies: Beta Gamma Sigma, 137; Phi Beta Kappa, 134
Hooper, Paul F., 154
Hoover, J. Edgar, 74
Hoshida, George, 58, 60–61, 65–66, 150n1, 150n13
Hughes, John Harold, 48
Hundred million defenders, 102

Iida, Kenkichi, 33–34
Inland Sea, 4, 7
Inouye, Daniel K., 144
Internment, hearing of J. S. Miwa, 42–53
Interrogation: "who will win?" (FBI), 51, 53; *Kempeitai,* (Military Police), 90
Iriye, Akira, 154
Irwin, Robert, 7
Issei, 34, 45–46, 60, 62, 68, 75

Japan: "invincible," 114; modernization of, 3–6, 12; militarization of, 19, 96
Japanese Army: Fifth Army Divison,

12, 38; officers, 93; Shozo Miwa, 100, 120
Japanese Chamber of Commerce, 30, 33–34, 36, 43, 49, 53, 61
Japanese consul, 9, 14, 34, 43, 49–53, 63, 69, 74, 83
Japanese Cultural Center of Hawai'i, ix, 149n2, 150n1, 150n9, 153–154
Japanese Exclusion Act, 24, 29, 44, 150n16
Japanese Surrender, 90, 116–117, 155; effect on Fumio Miwa, 108–109, 116–117, 121; Seigo's estimate, 79, 114
Japanese workers, 6–11, 13, 39, 62
Johnson, Byron L., 130, 134–135, 137

Kaiulani, Princess, 6
Kalākaua, King David, 5–7
Kaneko, Kay Uno, 155
Kashima, Tetsuden, 156
Kawai, Kazuo, 115, 117, 151nn1–3, 152n3, 152n6, 152nn8–9, 155
Kawamoto-Nishimoto, Michi, 155
Knaefler, Tomi Kaizawa, 151n32, 153
Koreans in Japan, 87
Koseki, 153
Kudo family: Binjiro, 34, 137; Yoko, 137–139, 143–146
Kure City, 120, 122–123
Kyodatsu, 117

LaFeber, Walter, 154
Langer, Elinor, 155
Lili'uokalani, Queen, 9
Loomis, Charles F., 35
Lordsburg Camp, 56–71
Luck: of Miwa family, ix, 147; of Kudo family, 137

M-Day legislation, 40
Manchukuo, 29, 89
Manchuria, 23, 29, 46, 50, 115, 137
Martial law, 41–44, 48, 52, 54–55, 73, 154
Marumoto, Masaji, 132
Marusan Rubber Company, 27–28, 32, 36, 141
Massie Case, 85
Matsunaga, Spark M., 146

Mayfield, I.H., 52
Mid-Pacific Institute, 24, 127–130
Migration: main pattern, 17; transnational, x, 26, 85
Military service: of Senkichi Miwa, 12, 14–15; of Shoso Miwa, 100, 120
Miwa, James Seigo, 23–83
Miwa, Lawrence Fumio, 83–147
Miwa, Marujiro, 3–12
Miwa, Senkichi, xi, 11–18
Miwa, Stephen, ix, 147–148
Miwa Street, xi, 31–32, 94, 111. *See also* Yokogawa
Miyamoto, Archie, 79, 151n34
Miyamoto, Kazuo, 45, 149n4
Model citizens, 134, 144
Mōʻiliʻili, 30
Moriyama, Alan Takeo, 149n2
Mozambique, 68, 78
Murakami, Robert, 132–134, 141

Native Hawaiian, 9–10, 15
New York University, 134
Niiya, Brian, 155
Nippu Jiji: incarceration of staff, 43; interview of J. S. Miwa, 34, 43, 53, 58. *See also* Soga, Yasutaro
Nisei, x, 34–37, 62–63, 146

Okabe, Reverend Jiro, 10
One Hundredth Battalion/442nd Regimental Combat Team, 146
Osaka, 31, 84–85, 137
Oshima, Kanesaburo, 64
Ota River, 4, 85, 100, 107, 111, 148
Ozaki, Otokichi, 54, 57, 61, 63–65, 150n1, 150n9, 151n29, 154

Pan Pacific Magazine, 34
Pan-Pacific Union, 24
Papaikou Plantation, 13
Pearl Harbor, 6, 41–42, 44, 51, 60, 65, 67, 89
Perry, Matthew, 3
Preyer, Bernard, 136–137, 144
Prisoner Exchange, 61, 66–78, 91, 141–142

Radiation, 115–116, 119–120, 131, 146
Religion: Buddhist, 43, 50, 63; Catholicism, 139; Christianity

24–25, 43, 46, 50; Shinto, 43, 50, 62, 92
Richards, Theodore, 24, 35
Rio de Janeiro, 68
Rogers, William P., 143
Roosevelt, Franklin D., 42, 66
Russo-Japanese War, 6, 14–15, 62

Saiki, Patsy Sumie, 150n7, 150n10, 150n13
Sakamoto, Pamela Rotner, 153
Samurai, impact of modernization, 3–5, 31, 79, 86, 116. *See also* Miwa, Marujiro
Sand Island Internment Camp, 45–46, 53–55, 61–63, 70
San Francisco, x, 15, 26, 30, 36, 46, 51, 71, 133
Santa Fe Internment Camp, 71–74
Sato, Katherine Miwa, 19–32, 69, 84–91, 93, 100, 110, 112, 114, 116–124, 127–129, 132–133, 145–146, 153, 156
Secret police of Japan, 29, 89–91, 141–143
Shibata, Yoshiro, 71
Shimada, Noriko, 154
Ship manifests, 36, 38–40, 154
Ships: Aramis, 78; Beutala, 9–10; Coolidge, 67; Gripsholm, 64, 74, 78; Gordon, 123–124; Maui, 55; *Tatsuta Maru,* 38–40, 67; *Teia Maru,* 78. *See also* Prisoner Exchange
Shivers, Robert L., 52
Shooting of internees. *See* Oshima
Short, Walter C., 37, 41
Singapore, 46, 68, 78–79
Sino-Japanese War, 14
Soga, Yasutaro, 56–63
Song of Tokko-tai, 101
Spanish-American War, 14
Special War Problems Agency, 66, 70, 73
Spector, Ronald H., 152n1, 155
Stone, Oliver E., 135–144
Stores (Miwa business), 16, 18–19, 26–28, 33, 48, 83–84
Sumida, Daizo, 33

Tadaima!, 100
Tengoku, 21

Territorial Food Committee (of
    Hawai'i), 40–42, 48
Tojo, Hideki, 92
Tokyo, 19, 34, 123
Tolstoy, Leo, 113
Tonomura (Village), 96
Toyoda, Sakichi, 100–102
Truman, Harry S., 133
Tsukiyama, Wilfred C., 35

U.S. Army Intelligence, 37, 42, 44,
    52

Weaver, Galen, 35
World War I, 18
World War II, 89

Yamato damashii, 92
Yasui, Minoru, 133
YMCA, 35, 43
Yokogawa, xi, 27, 31–33, 79, 85,
    89, 92, 94, 100, 105, 107–108,
    111–112, 141, 145, 153
Yokohama Specie Bank, 50, 57
Yoshida, Shigeo, 36

ABOUT THE AUTHOR

Tom Coffman is a political reporter who evolved into writing books and directing historical documentaries. Previous books include the widely read *Catch a Wave*, a political case study; *Nation Within*, a history of America's occupation of Hawai'i; *The Island Edge of America*, a twentieth-century political history; and *I Respectfully Dissent*, a biography of a distinguished labor lawyer and jurist Edward H. Nakamura. His numerous films include *First Battle* about the struggle for equality in wartime Hawai'i; *Arirang: The Korean American Journey*; *Nation Within*; and *Ninoy Aquino and the Rise of People Power*. Coffman is a three-time recipient of the Hawaii Book Publishers Association's award for nonfiction writing, and for his cumulative work he received the Hawai'i Award for Literature. His work has been read and screened widely throughout the Pacific and the United States.